COSTA RICA

Erin Foley & Barbara Cooke

Marshall Cavendish
Benchmark
New York

PICTURE CREDITS

Cover photo: © Jeffrey Arguedas/ epa/ CORBIS

alt.TYPE/REUTERS: 9, 25, 30, 41, 114 • Audrius Tomonois: 135 • Bjorn Klingwall: 38 • Buddy Mays: 6, 51, 58, 72, 104 • Chip & Rosa Maria Peterson: 3, 76, 82, 126 • Corbis: 29, 86 • David Simson: 65, 97 • DDB Stock Photo: 8, 12, 17, 19, 22, 28, 30, 37, 46, 47, 48, 60, 61, 64, 73, 75, 78, 83, 88, 95, 101, 105, 106, 111, 121, 122, 123, 127 • Focus Team, Italy: 10, 15, 18, 36, 49, 57, 74, 107, 125 • Hulton Deutsch: 24, 27 • Hutchinson: 117 • Image bank: 16, 129 • Jason Laure: 66 • Lonely Planet Images: 55, 71 • MCIA/Richard Lee: 130 • National Geographic Image Collection: 53 • Photolibrary: 1,5, 50, 56, 67, 70, 77, 79, 93, 96, 102, 103, 108, 120 • Pietro Scozzari: 4, 20, 42, 59, 80, 81, 84, 102, 110 • South American Pictures: 14, 40, 43, 45, 62, 68, 77, 85, 87, 99, 113, 119 • Stockfood/Bischof, Harry: 131 • Victor Englebert: 11, 13, 91, 98, 100

PRECEDING PAGE

Rural schoolboys having a game of soccer.

Publisher (U.S.): Michelle Bisson
Editors: Deborah Grahame, Mabelle Yeo, Stephanie Pee, Crystal Ouyang
Copyreader: Daphne Hougham
Designers: Jailani Basari, Rachel Chen
Picture researchers: Thomas Khoo, Joshua Ang

Marshall Cavendish Benchmark
99 White Plains Road
Tarrytown, NY 10591
Web site: www.marshallcavendish.us

© Times Editions Private Limited 1996
© Marshall Cavendish International (Asia) Private Limited 2008
All rights reserved. First edition 1996. Second edition 2008.
® "Cultures of the World" is a registered trademark of Times Publishing Limited.

Originated and designed by Times Editions
An imprint of Marshall Cavendish International (Asia) Private Limited
A member of Times Publishing Limited

All Internet sites were correct and accurate at the time of printing. All monetary figures in this publication are in U.S. dollars.

Library of Congress Cataloging-in-Publication Data

Foley, Erin, 1967–
    Costa Rica / by Erin Foley & Barbara Cooke. — 2nd ed.
        p. cm. — (Cultures of the world)
    Summary: "Provides comprehensive information on the geography, history, wildlife, governmental structure, economy, cultural diversity, peoples, religion, and culture of Costa Rica"—Provided by publisher.
    Includes bibliographical references and index.
        ISBN 978-0-7614-2079-8
    1. Costa Rica—Juvenile literature. I. Cooke, Barbara, 1966– II. Title. III. Series.
    F1543.2.F65 2007
    972.86—dc22   2006101736

Printed in China
9 8 7 6 5 4 3 2 1

CONTENTS

A fruit vendor in a poor neighborhood of San José.

Beautiful stained glass windows like this are common in many cathedrals and churches across Costa Rica.

INTRODUCTION

COSTA RICA MAY BE a small country, but it stands out among its Central American neighbors as a paradise of natural beauty and a nation that enjoys general peace, stability, and prosperity. A country that remains true to its ideals, it is one of the oldest democracies in the region and one of the few countries in the world that has abolished its military, preferring instead to invest in education for its people. Home to one of the world's richest and most diverse natural environments, Costa Rica has also set an outstanding example in its approach to conservation.

For its relatively homogenous population of mostly Spanish descent, life is a balance of tradition and progress. Costa Ricans, who refer to themselves as Ticos (TEE-kohs), strive to get on in life through hard work and education, yet continue to respect conservative values, especially when it comes to family matters. Costa Rica is a country celebrated for its extraordinary beauty and for a people distinguished by their warmth and sincerity.

GEOGRAPHY

THE REPUBLIC OF COSTA RICA, with a land area of 19,730 square miles (51,100 square km), is the third smallest country in Central America after El Salvador and Belize. It is slightly smaller than the state of West Virginia. Costa Rica is situated between 8° and 11° north of the equator, extending from the northwest to the southeast along the lower portion of the Central American isthmus.

It is bordered by the countries of Nicaragua to the north and Panama to the south and southeast, and by the Caribbean Sea to the northeast and the Pacific Ocean to the west and southwest. Its Caribbean coast is only 135 miles (217 km) long, while its Pacific coastline stretches nearly 780 miles (1,255 km). At its broadest point the country extends to approximately 174 miles (280 km) from coast to coast, while narrowing to less than 75 miles (120 km) across at its narrowest point.

Opposite: **A waterfall in the rain forest in Corcovado National Park, located in the Osa Peninsula.**

TOPOGRAPHY AND GEOLOGY

Two major mountain chains, running from the northwest to southeast, constitute the interior highlands of Costa Rica: the Cordillera Volcánica, which starts in the northwest, and the Cordillera de Talamanca in the south. The word *cordillera* means "mountain range." As suggested by its name, the Cordillera Volcánica includes several volcanoes.

IRAZÚ'S ERUPTION

Irazú erupted dramatically in 1963 after 20 years of slumber, while the U.S. president, John F. Kennedy, was visiting Costa Rica. It blanketed the capital city of San José with 5 inches (13 cm) of muddy ash and destroyed crops and large numbers of cattle. Although it was a disaster for the economy, the huge deposit of volcanic ash enriched the soil of the Meseta Central (Central Valley) for decades thereafter. Irazú last erupted in 1994.

The smoking crater of Poás Volcano.

It is not unusual to feel tremors regularly in Costa Rica. During a two-month period in 1989 seismologists recorded more than 16,000 tremors, although only 16 of them registered above 4.0 on the Richter scale.

The Cordillera Volcánica actually consists of three continuous mountain ranges: the northwestern Cordillera de Guanacaste, the smaller Cordillera Tilarán, and the Cordillera Central. The de Guanacaste and the Central chains both include several volcanic peaks. Two of the volcanoes in the Cordillera Central—Poás at 8,870 feet (2,704 m) and Irazú at 11,257 feet (3,431 m)—are still active.

Near the middle of the country, the northern point of the Cordillera de Talamanca begins parallel to the southernmost point of the Cordillera Central. Their highland elevations merge to form the Central Valley, which historically has attracted the greatest number of inhabitants.

The Cordillera de Talamanca includes the Chirripó Grande, the highest point in Costa Rica at 12,530 feet (3,819 m).

EARTHQUAKES Costa Rica is located along a geological fault system where the Pacific Ocean's Cocos plate meets the tectonic plate underlying the Caribbean. The country is therefore subject to occasional and sometimes devastating earthquakes.

Several recent earthquakes have affected Costa Rica in varying degrees. The most recent occurred on November 20, 2004, just outside San José, the capital of Costa Rica. It was not quite as strong as the one that hit the Caribbean town of Pandora in 1991 that measured 7.4 on the Richter scale—the strongest earthquake felt in Costa Rica since 1910, which killed 1,750 people. The 1991 quake caused only superficial structural damage in San José, 70 miles (113 km) away, but wreaked devastation on the Caribbean coastal areas. Although only 27 people were reported killed, more than 400 people were injured and 13,000 left homeless.

The 1991 earthquake permanently changed Costa Rica's landscape. The port city of Puerto Limón, for instance, rose in elevation by almost 5 feet (1.5 m), as did other parts of the coastline. As a result, some canals are now too high to connect with the Atlantic Ocean. The quake also raised coral reefs in some places, killing the live coral exposed to the air and leaving only skeletal remains jutting out of the water.

Costa Rica's western limits are defined by the Pacific coast.

GEOGRAPHICAL REGIONS

Three main geographical regions define Costa Rica: the Pacific coastal area, the central highlands and the Caribbean lowlands. The narrow Pacific coastal region rises steeply into the central highlands, which then descend more gradually into the Caribbean plain. Tropical rain forests thrive in several Caribbean coastal areas in addition to the southern Pacific slopes.

PACIFIC COAST The Pacific lowlands are characterized by steep cliffs and narrow white-sand beaches. The coastline broadens into three peninsulas. The northernmost peninsula, the Nicoya Peninsula, juts to the southeast to form the Gulf of Nicoya. The southern Costa Rican peninsula, Osa, likewise, forms the Gulf of Dulce. The southern boundary runs through a narrow third peninsula, which terminates in Punta Burica. An alluvial (matter deposited by running water) coastal plain runs from the Osa Peninsula to the port of Puntarenas in the Gulf of Nicoya. Steep coastal mountain cliffs break the otherwise monotonous landscape of the coastal plains, whose northern end widens into the Valle de Tempisque.

CENTRAL HIGHLANDS The Central Valley is formed at the point where the southeastern end of the Cordillera Central runs parallel to the northwestern point of the Cordillera de Talamanca. The major portion of the Central Valley consists of two smaller basins making up the populous Meseta Central. Almost two-thirds of the population of Costa Rica inhabits this temperate area of about 3,900 square miles (10,100 square km).

Influenced by the Caribbean climate, the Cartago basin to the east has heavier rainfall and higher humidity, in spite of its higher elevation of about 4,930 feet (1,503 m) above sea level. The San José basin lies northwest of Cartago. Costa Rica's capital city, San José, and its sprawling suburbs are located here. With a more temperate climate and elevation of approximately 3,773 feet (1,150 m), the San José basin produces much of Costa Rica's cash crop, coffee. Another large basin, the General Valley, lies to the south. Until the 1940s this area was relatively isolated. The construction of the Pan-American Highway after World War II, however, opened up the area to farmers.

Many tropical cloud forests are found at higher elevations, from approximately 3,300 feet to 9,800 feet (1,000 m to 3,000 m). In these very high environments clouds continually drench the forest with a fine mist, nourishing a variety of plants such as orchids and ferns. The Monteverde Cloud Forest Reserve in Costa Rica, the largest cloud forest in Central America, has been preserved as a national park. The *páramo* (PAH-rah-moh), a special, treeless environment with sparse, hardy grasses, like a moor, spreads across the highest elevations, above 9,800 feet (3,000 m).

The Reventazón River, a favorite of white water rafters, is characterized by its lush, natural terrain and a heavily forested gorge.

CARIBBEAN LOWLANDS Costa Rica's Caribbean coast is made up of lowlands that extend into much of the northern and inland areas of the country. This region is a geographical continuation of the broad lowlands of Nicaragua and has an average elevation of less than 400 feet (120 m) above sea level. The Caribbean coast is lined with numerous white- and black-sand (from crushed lava flow) beaches, while the Caribbean lowlands constitute nearly one-fifth of Costa Rica's total land area. The region consists mainly of flat plains irrigated by streams flowing from the central highlands. The lowlands in the north also have a scattering of hills and volcanoes.

RIVERS

Costa Rica is well irrigated by many rivers and streams. Most of the rivers have sources in the central highlands and flow into either the Caribbean Sea or Pacific Ocean. Several of the rivers have been harnessed for hydroelectric power, and many also provide the main source of transportation through isolated areas by riverboat and canoe. The principal Pacific-flowing rivers include the Río Grande de Tárcoles and the Río Grande de Térraba, which is fed by tributaries rising out of the General Valley. The main rivers flowing to the Caribbean Sea include the Reventazón and the San Juan. The San Juan River originates from Lake Nicaragua, within Nicaragua, and forms a major part of the international boundary with that country.

CLIMATE AND SEASONS

Given its proximity to the equator, Costa Rica is a tropical country. Its climate, however, varies according to elevation and, to a lesser degree, to the amount of annual rainfall in different locations. The average temperature on the coast varies from about 77°F to 90°F (25°C to 32°C), while the average temperature in the highlands is 72°F (22°C).

There are two definite seasons: *verano* (veh-RAH-noh) and *invierno* (een-vee-AIR-noh). These terms are often loosely translated as "summer" and "winter," respectively. In Costa Rica, *verano* refers specifically to the dry season and *invierno* to the rainy season.

Unlike North America, Costa Rica experiences summer, or the dry season, at the end of the year and winter, or the wet season, in the middle of the year. The rainy season generally lasts from April or May through October or November. September and October tend to have the heaviest rainfall, when several days may pass with no interruption in the downpour. The *verano* usually begins around mid-November, signaling the coffee harvest and Christmas season.

Above: **Lush rain forest near Puerto Limón.**

Opposite: **Carara National Park, located near Costa Rica's Pacific coast.**

FLORA

Costa Rica has 12 distinct ecological zones, with an incredibly diverse range of plant and animal life. The government is committed to preserving the country's natural beauty and resources through a system of national parks. Costa Rica has received numerous international awards for its conservation efforts. Nonetheless, its conservation laws are often violated: Costa Rica still experiences rapid deforestation, especially outside the national parks and reserves.

Because of its tropical location and variety of ecological zones, including both tropical rain forests and tropical dry forests, Costa Rica is bursting with botanical variety. About 20 percent of the country is covered with forests of broadleaf evergreen trees, such as oak, mahogany, and tropical cedar trees. There are over 2,000 distinct species of trees and 9,000 kinds of flowering plants, including more than 1,200 species of Costa Rica's national flower, the orchid.

TROPICAL DRY FORESTS The tropical dry forests do not receive rain during the *verano* and are vulnerable to accidental fires. As the drought ends in April, the leafy trees—including the purple jacaranda, pink and white meadow oak, and bright orange flame-of-the-forest— explode into bursts of colors. Because of the lack of moisture for six months of the year, tropical dry forests are not as densely forested as tropical rain forests. These arid zones have only two basic layers: the treetops and ground-level bushes.

TROPICAL RAIN FOREST While the dry forests have sparse vegetation and only two layers, tropical rain forests are densely packed with several layers of plant and animal life. Each layer, from the treetop canopy to the ground floor of the forest, provides a suitable habitat for different forms of life. Humidity is high due to year-round rain, long hours of sunlight, and high temperatures. This mix of environmental factors creates ideal conditions for the proliferation of innumerable types of fungi, molds, ferns, vines, trees, and bushes.

COASTAL VEGETATION The coastal areas are characterized by palm trees or, in certain areas, by mangroves. Mangroves choke portions of the shoreline, especially along the Nicoya and Dulce gulfs, with their interlocking, stiltlike roots. Costa Rica is home to five different species of the mangrove, a tree uniquely adapted to surviving in salty coastal habitats. Their shallow roots draw nutrients from the surface of their swampy surroundings, while patches of spongy tissue on their bark enable them to absorb oxygen from the air. While palm trees are prolific along the Caribbean coast, they have also been transplanted to the Pacific lowlands, where plantations of African palms have been established.

Some orchids are so minuscule that they measure less than a millimeter in diameter. Others have hanging petals that are more than 1.5 feet (46 cm) long. The majority of orchids are epiphytes, taking root on trees or other plants, although in a nonparasitic fashion. One biologist reportedly found 47 different species growing on a single tree.

FAUNA

The country's many ecological zones also foster an astounding variety of animal, insect, and bird life, which can be attributed to Costa Rica's unique location as a bridge between North and South America.

AMPHIBIANS AND REPTILES Costa Rica has an estimated 160 species of amphibians and more than 200 species of reptiles, over half of which are snakes, including some venomous vipers like the fer-de-lance and bushmaster. Most of the amphibian species are frogs and toads, many of which are brightly colored. The most commonly spotted reptile is the harmless green iguana, which can grow to more than 6 feet (1.8 m) long. Both land-dwelling and aquatic turtles found in the Caribbean lowlands

The venom from poison arrow frogs is used by indigenous people to coat the tips of their arrows.

were once common but are now critically endangered. Crocodiles and their smaller relatives, the caiman, inhabit the wet lowlands of both coasts.

MAMMALS Costa Rica is home to about 200 species of mammals, half of which are bats. Many species have been hunted to extinction, while others remain endangered. Habitat destruction due to deforestation poses the most threat to the jaguar, the largest and most powerful member of the American cat family. The tapir is also under fire due to overhunting. Most of those remaining are now only found in areas where hunting is restricted.

BIRDS More than 850 species of birds have been identified in Costa Rica. The endangered resplendent quetzal—a sacred bird for the ancient Mayas and Aztecs who once lived in Central America—and scarlet macaw are considered the "rare jewels" of the country; fortunately, both are plentiful in the protected reserves. Other colorful birds include the laughing falcon, tanager, blue-footed booby, and six different species of the toucan.

INSECTS Although several thousand known species of insects inhabit Costa Rica, many more remain unidentified. The blue morpho butterfly, tarantulas, and leaf-cutter ants are just some of the insects that are found. The country has thousands of species of ants and more species of butterflies than all of Africa. For example, on a single tree in the rain forest, entomologists (scientists who study insects) have collected over 950 species of beetles.

Birds such as this colorful macaw are numerous in the wet lowlands of the country.

The growth of San José as a city was fueled by Costa Rica's booming coffee exports at the end of the 19th century.

CITIES

Costa Rica has six major urban areas: San José, Cartago, Heredia, and Alajuela, which constitute the four colonial cities of the Central Valley; Puntarenas on the Pacific coast; and Puerto Limón on the Caribbean Sea. About two-thirds of the country's population of 4 million lives in the Central Valley.

SAN JOSÉ The capital city dominates national life in Costa Rica. It is the political, cultural, and economic center of the country. In the early 1940s its population was only 70,000 and villages and coffee groves surrounded the city. After World War II, increasing numbers of people migrated from the rural areas to the capital in search of better-paying jobs. The city sprawled outward in all directions incorporating surrounding villages and coffee fields into the suburbs of San José. Unfortunately, this urban sprawl occurred with no planning or zoning. The basic infrastructure lagged behind the new growth, and even today, streets, water supply, and sewage disposal are often inadequate or nonexistent. However, suburbs, especially those around San Pedro, are tranquil and have a supply of potable water. Low- and middle-income neighborhoods, shantytowns, and fashionable neighborhoods are often erected side by side.

In the midst of the modern concrete architecture of San José, historic structures, such as the National Theater, remain. Most were built in the latter part of the 19th century or the early part of the 20th century. Most colonial-era architecture has not survived the major earthquakes.

18

Josefinos (ho-say FEE-nohs), as San José residents are known, number about 340,000. With the inclusion of the outlying areas, the population now reaches about 1.2 million. The downtown area is congested with cars, and pedestrians spill onto the streets because the sidewalks are often cracked and broken or packed with vendors. The air is filled with diesel and gas fumes, and the constant din of motor vehicles, shouting vendors, and ongoing construction can be overwhelming. In spite of its urban congestion, San José still attracts tourists and residents with its vibrant nightlife, national symphony orchestra, museums, art galleries, restaurants, and an international flavor.

Fishing boats gathering at a bay in Puerto Limón.

PUNTARENAS This city of about 100,000 people is situated on the Gulf of Nicoya. It was the principal port on the Pacific coast until the deepwater port, Puerto Caldera, was constructed about 10 miles (16 km) to the south. Today, fishing constitutes the primary occupation and industry of Puntarenas.

PUERTO LIMÓN The city of Limón is Costa Rica's principal port city and is its most important city on the Caribbean coast, with a population that numbers around 90,000. Regrettably, it is one of the poorest and most neglected areas of the country. Puerto Limón achieved prominence during the latter half of the 19th century as an export center for coffee and bananas being shipped to European markets.

HISTORY

THE HISTORY OF COSTA RICA usually starts with the humble beginnings of its Spanish settlers and progresses to its relatively prosperous present-day status. Settlers worked their own plots of land, and gradually a poor but proud and self-reliant society emerged. Thus the image of the yeoman farmer is imprinted on Costa Rica's national consciousness. On the other hand, 33 of the 44 presidents from 1821 to 1970 were direct descendents of three of the original colonizers of the country who were of noble blood. However, archaeologists have found evidence suggesting the existence of civilizations in Costa Rica as far back as 10,000 years ago. By the time the Europeans arrived, they found five main indigenous groups dwelling there.

Costa Ricans take great pride in Costa Rica's long democratic tradition. In contrast to the tumultuous history of most of its neighbors, Costa Ricans have generally managed to avoid violent political and social upheavals.

PRE-COLUMBIAN TIMES

Historically, the territory of present-day Costa Rica was sparsely populated in comparison with other areas of Central America. At the time of the Spanish conquest in the 16th century, more than 25,000 Indians lived in the area. They were broadly divided into five groups: the Chorotega, Carib, Boruca, Corobicí, and Nahua. Rather than uniting, they constantly fought for control of the territory. When victorious, they exacted tribute from their vanquished enemies in the form of gold and prisoners, whom they used as slaves or as offerings in ritual sacrifice. Many of their religious ceremonies and crafts reflected Mayan influence.

The indigenous inhabitants fiercely resisted the Spanish invasion. Some fled into the rain forest; from there they continued to resist Spanish rule long after colonization.

Indigenous Indians used beans as currency and spun cotton into threads for weaving cloth. They were also skilled metalworkers, crafting ornaments and other objects from gold that they imported from other regions.

Opposite: **Located in San José, Costa Rica's Central Post Office is one of the oldest buildings in the country.**

Detail from a mural by Luís Ferón (1940) in the Salon Dorado at the Museum of Costa Rican Art, depicting Christopher Columbus arriving at Costa Rica in 1502.

SPANISH CONQUEST

Christopher Columbus was the first European to set foot on the coast of what is now Costa Rica. On his fourth voyage to the Americas, on September 18, 1502, he landed at Cariay, the site of today's Caribbean Puerto Limón. Columbus established friendly relations with the Indians, who greeted him with gifts of gold. Spanish adventurers were later drawn to the area in their search for gold. Successive explorers began to think of this area as "the rich coast," and thus called it Costa Rica. The larger area—present-day Costa Rica, Panama, and yet unexplored parts of the isthmus—was called Veragua.

The Spanish colonized much of what is now Central America, forming several provinces. However, they found the indigenous groups of Costa Rica difficult to subdue. The impenetrable jungle and new diseases that were native to Costa Rica further impeded their conquest. Their efforts were not helped by their constant infighting, as different groups competed with each other to find gold. In 1539 the area of Costa Rica was separated from Veragua and officially named Costa Rica.

It was not until 1561 that Juan de Cavallón succeeded in colonizing the Caribbean coast of Costa Rica. He established the settlement of Garcimuñoz in 1561, but he left in 1562, discouraged by the lack of gold. Juan Vásquez de Coronado replaced him as governor of Costa Rica, and in 1564 he relocated the base settlement to the fertile highlands and named it Cartago. The new settlement provided an agricultural base to sustain further exploration and colonization of the territory.

COLONIAL PERIOD

In 1573 the Spanish crown fixed permanent boundaries for Costa Rica, which still had only two settlements, Cartago and Aranjuez. The territory, physically isolated from the rest of Central America, stagnated as one of the most backward and neglected possessions of the Spanish-American empire. During the Spanish conquest the Native American Indians were driven out of their traditional territories and many were killed as a result of ongoing warfare between indigenous groups, attacks from the Spanish invaders, rampant new diseases introduced by the Spanish, and starvation.

Many of the surviving Indians became Christians, especially the Chorotegas. As Christians, they were allowed to remain in their own villages under their traditional leaders if they wished, or they could move into the Hispanic settlements, where they intermarried and were quickly assimilated into the mestizo (mixed blood) population. The only remaining purely Native American population isolated itself in the Talamanca region.

Within a few generations after the conquest, the Costa Rican population had assumed a generally mestizo character that identified completely with Spanish culture. The small number of black slaves that the Spanish originally brought to the territory integrated into the Hispanic community along with most of the Indians. As was the case in other parts of Latin America, the Spanish settlers forced the indigenous people into servitude during the late 16th and early 17th centuries. This system failed in the long run in Costa Rica, however, because the local population was too small to exploit as a labor force. The settler population also grew slowly, as the country yielded no mineral or other native resources and was relatively unattractive to most immigrants.

The hidalgos, or gentry of Costa Rican society, were not wealthy compared with the gentry of other Central American societies. More often than not, they were the sons of poor Spanish families who came to America to seek their fortunes. In Costa Rica, they ended up as farmers who enjoyed certain privileges because of their family name. For instance, only the hidalgos were allowed to serve on the municipal councils, and they received a deference from the plebeyos, or commoners.

Spanish rule in the early 1500s was extensive. The picture shows Columbus being taken prisoner of state after establishing a Spanish settlement at Hispaniola (Haiti and the Dominican Republic). The settlers had protested against living conditions, the lack of gold, and alleged atrocities, and Columbus was sent back to Spain. On his release, he set out on his fourth voyage and arrived at the site of Puerto Limón in Costa Rica.

Costa Rican society at that time was made up of two basic social classes. The hidalgos formed the ruling class and were called by the honorary titles of don, or sir, or doña, or madam. The commoners were collectively known as *plebeyos* (play-BAY-yohs), literally translated as plebeians. The settlers, hidalgos and *plebeyos* alike, worked their own lands, which made it difficult for anyone to amass large holdings. In this aspect Costa Rica was unique among its Central American neighbors.

Thus Costa Rica started out as a very poor colony without great economic opportunities for its settlers. On the other hand, the poverty of its landholders, combined with the lack of a large underclass, gave rise to a more equitable class structure than any that existed in Spain and in most of the other Spanish colonies.

TOWARD INDEPENDENCE

By the early 1800s the Spanish empire had been weakened because of Napoleon Bonaparte's conquest of Spain. First, in August 1821, Mexico declared independence. Costa Rica was governed by proxy by Guatemala, which had been the Spanish administrative center, as part of the Capitanía General de Guatemala. Thus when Guatemala unilaterally declared the independence of all the Central American provinces, Costa Rica gained its independence as well. The Costa Ricans were initially unsure whether they should remain loyal to the crown or declare independence, too, so the municipal councils of the four principal towns of Heredia, Cartago, Alajuela, and San José met separately to try to decide.

CENTRAL AMERICAN FEDERATION While the Costa Ricans were waiting to decide their future, the newly proclaimed "emperor" of Mexico demanded that the Central American provinces submit to his authority. Again, the principal Costa Rican towns were divided in their response. Heredia and Cartago voted to unite with an imperialist Mexico, while Alajuela and San José rejected Mexico in favor of either uniting with another Central American province or becoming an independent republic. This conflict sparked a civil war between the towns in December 1822. After a one-day battle the republican forces from Alajuela and San José defeated the imperialist troops from Heredia and Cartago.

In March 1823 Costa Rica finally declared its independence from Spain. Five months later Costa Rica joined with the United Provinces of Central America, also known as the Central American Federation. However, competing interests and civil war prevented its effectiveness. Although the federation existed for only 16 years, it stood as a symbol of regional unification that many Central Americans still desire.

Independence hero Simón Bolívar hoped for the unification of Latin America. However, the Central American Federation was doomed to collapse as it was torn by war and strife. Costa Rica withdrew its membership in 1829 but reentered the union nine months later. The entire federation disintegrated within a decade, nevertheless, and was officially disbanded in February 1839.

YOUNG NATIONHOOD   During the 1830s Costa Rica was again torn by conflict as the principal towns competed to be the capital. In 1834 the newly elected head of state, Braulio Carrillo Colina, established San José as the capital, which provoked a rebellion by the other three towns. In 1838 Carrillo lost his bid for reelection; however, he immediately seized control of the government as a dictator. Three years later he abolished the constitution and declared himself dictator for life. During his four-year dictatorship he took steps to advance the political and economic interests of Costa Rica. In addition to reorganizing the government and establishing a new legal code, he also encouraged the development of the coffee industry, at the same time encouraging an increase in the number of small landholders. In 1842 Carrillo was overthrown by his opponents and a few years of instability followed.

In 1847 the congress appointed José María Castro Madriz as the first official president. In 1848 he formally declared Costa Rica an independent republic and approved a reform constitution, leading to his being called the "Founder of the Republic." The new constitution, like those before it, was inspired by the European enlightenment. It confirmed the right to freedom of expression and association, and emphasized the importance of education. Suffrage, however, was limited to men who were literate and owned property.

In 1849 Castro Madriz was forced to resign by a coalition of coffee barons and disgruntled army officers who opposed his reform policies and his inability to quell rising unrest. He was succeeded by Juan Rafael Mora Porras, a coffee planter and member of an important political family.

COFFEE IS KING   Coffee had been introduced near the end of the 18th century. By 1829 it was the country's primary source of foreign exchange. It was vigorously promoted by dictator Carrillo and President Castro Madriz. Carrillo offered free land to anyone who agreed to plant coffee, and he constructed roads for transporting the harvested beans to market.

By the mid-1800s a small group of prosperous coffee growers, although only modestly wealthy in comparison with other Latin American elites, was able to influence the government to keep taxes low and to promote the coffee trade. Fortunately, this politically powerful elite did not use its influence to oppress the underclass. Rather, the government enacted policies to develop education and public works, in the belief that an educated and well-off populace would lead to greater progress and prosperity for all. This enlightened self-interest inspired the coffee barons to reinvest the profits of their international trade, financing improvements within Costa Rica.

WILLIAM WALKER In 1855 a political faction in neighboring Nicaragua hired William Walker, an American adventurer from Tennessee, to overthrow Nicaragua's president. After deposing the incumbent, however, Walker seized the presidency for himself. He reintroduced slavery in Nicaragua.

Outraged by this infringement of national sovereignty, Costa Rican president Mora Porras declared war on Walker and his regime in February 1856. Mora Porras was able to raise an army of some 9,000 men, which Walker confronted with several hundred of his mercenaries. The Costa Ricans attacked Walker's forces in the town of Rivas, across the Nicaraguan border. A drummer boy by the name of Juan Santamaría succeeded in setting fire

William Walker, an adventurer from the United States, proclaimed himself ruler of Nicaragua in 1856. Costa Rica's outrage at his action resulted in the Battle of Rivas.

to Walker's stronghold, driving his men out from their cover. Santamaría lost his life in the ensuing action, but is remembered as a national hero in Costa Rica.

Other Central American troops soon joined Costa Rica and defeated Walker in April 1857. The war against Walker, nevertheless, was very costly to Costa Rica. Almost half the Costa Rican troops died, either in battle or from disease or poor conditions in the military camps. Even with its enormous losses, the war became an event of great national pride and importance. While Costa Rica had previously been split by regional interests, the war united the country and inspired a sense of national unity.

ECONOMIC PROGRESS, SETBACK FOR DEMOCRACY Although the glory of victory shone on President Mora Porras for a brief time, the high cost of that victory ultimately led to his overthrow. More than a decade later, in 1870, the presidency was again overthrown, this time by General Tomás Guardia Gutiérrez, who quickly assumed dictatorial powers and ruled until his death in 1882.

While he restricted civil liberties, Guardia Gutiérrez tried to redistribute land and wealth. He also modernized the country, improving public schools, sanitation and public works, and the transportation network. He incurred a large national debt, however, which took the country several decades to repay.

The monument to national hero Juan Santamaría.

Guardia Gutiérrez's greatest contribution to Costa Rica may have been the railroad project that he initiated in 1871. He hired American Minor Cooper Keith to build a railroad from the Meseta Central to the Caribbean coast, connecting the cities of Alajuela and Puerto Limón. Immigrant labor, mostly from Italy, China, and Jamaica, helped to complete the 20-year project. Some 4,000 lives were lost from injuries and disease in the construction project, which cost about $8 million, but the railroad contributed greatly to Costa Rica's economic development. The railroad also attracted foreign entrepreneurs and opened up the Pacific coast. It also encouraged the growth of the banana industry. The banana industry was dominated by foreign companies, owned primarily by North American businessmen. This meant that the profits generated from the export of bananas were not kept within Costa Rica. A major banana export company was Minor Keith's United Fruit Company, established in 1899. It controlled large areas of land and was very involved in Costa Rican politics. It also provided the impetus for the practice of legal racial segregation in Costa Rica between Hispanic workers and workers of African descent.

The construction of the railroad opened up Costa Rica and saw the proliferation of banana plantations and trade.

Over the next few decades Costa Rica became more democratic. Voting rights were expanded, but elections in the 1920s and 1930s were built upon a system of personalized political patronage, and rival liberals ruled the presidency for 12 years. The liberal philosophy opposed taxation on personal wealth and desired a limited role for a government freed from influence by the Church and widespread opportunities for education.

CIVIL WAR AND THE 1948 "REVOLUTION"

By the 1930s Costa Rica's long emphasis on the benefits of education produced a more politically astute citizenry and a relatively large middle class. This increased political awareness, however, prompted people to join various interest groups. City workers, farmers, and the urban middle class organized strikes as well as demonstrations in attempts to influence national policies. Suffrage for women and illiterates alike was introduced, and citizenship was conferred on all who were born in Costa Rica, meaning that Afro-Caribbeans born there were finally made citizens of Costa Rica.

Former president Rafael Angel Calderón Guardia expanded the role of the state in providing for its people's needs.

THE CALDERÓN PRESIDENCY Rafael Angel Calderón Guardia was elected in 1941 through the powerful backing of the National Republican Party, which represented politicians and bureaucrats. His administration was marked by genuine social and economic reforms, such as reconciliation between church and state and an attempt to amend the constitution to allow a greater role for the government in certain issues. Many liberals, however, became outraged by Calderón's promulgation of the Social Guarantee amendments and by his expropriation of immigrant-owned properties during World War II. The Social Guarantees were a set of 15 constitutional amendments that allowed congress to legislate such measures as a labor code, social security, health insurance, and the right of squatters to obtain titles to uncommitted land that they had cultivated.

BORDER CONFLICTS

The beginning of the 20th century marked a period of ongoing conflicts with Costa Rica's neighbors, Nicaragua and Panama. In 1916 Costa Rica protested an agreement between Nicaragua and the United States. The agreement gave the United States the perpetual right to build a canal across the isthmus through Nicaraguan territory, using Costa Rica's portion of the San Juan River. Although the Central American court sided with Costa Rica, the United States and Nicaragua ignored the judgment—thereby discrediting the court and ultimately causing its dissolution.

Costa Rica also had a long-standing border dispute with Panama concerning the definition of the boundary through the Sixaola basin on the Caribbean coast. In 1900 the French president arbitrated the dispute and awarded the area to Panama. Costa Rica protested. In 1914 the chief justice of the U.S. Supreme Court arbitrated and awarded the area to Costa Rica—raising a protest from Panama. In 1921 the dispute escalated into armed hostilities when Costa Rica attempted to expel Panamanian residents in the Coto region on the Pacific coast. The United States intervened and evacuated the Panamanians. Relations between Costa Rica and Panama were broken off until an agreement was reached in 1941, ceding much of the disputed area to Costa Rica.

CIVIL WAR BREAKS OUT Amid rising political and civil unrest, the 1948 election was the most divisive election the country had ever experienced. Otilio Ulate Blanco represented the National Union Party and was supported by the newly established Social Democratic Party. Ulate won by 10,000 votes against Calderón, who was seeking reelection through the National Republican Party. Each side accused the other of fraud, forcing the Election Commission to examine the issue. While two members of the commission upheld Ulate's victory, the third member disagreed, so the sitting president demanded that the legislature decide the election. The congress, which was filled with Calderón supporters, annulled the election altogether and appointed Calderón as president.

But Ulate refused to concede defeat, and an armed force of volunteers was quickly assembled on his behalf. The head of this army, José Figueres Ferrer, was a landowner who had been exiled for two years for publicly opposing Calderón's policies in 1942. He gathered about 600 men, mostly students and the sons of farmers, to form the National Liberation Army. On March 12, 1948, the civil war began, but the government was ill prepared to defend itself. The revolutionaries won the monthlong war, calling it the War of National Liberation. A pact was signed by the two sides on April 19, 1948.

The civil war was the bloodiest period in Costa Rica's history. About 2,000 people lost their lives, with many more wounded during the battle.

THE MODERN PERIOD

After the civil war José Figueres was installed as president of a temporary ruling junta, or council. He called this body the Founding Junta of the Second Republic, to contrast it with the "failed" first republic. Figueres agreed that, after an interim period of 18 months, he would hand over the reins of government to the elected president, Otilio Ulate. During the brief period that it governed, the junta executed emergency decrees, nationalized the banks, and established a tax on wealth to help pay for repairs necessitated by the war. It extended voting rights to women and streamlined the system of Social Guarantees set up by Calderón.

Figueres also established an electoral system that eliminated the traditional system of political patronage to gain office and established the modern Costa Rican democracy in which political parties compete in fair and honest elections and then peacefully transfer power from one administration to the next.

The junta confronted repeated counterrevolutionary threats from supporters of Calderón, who were known as *calderonistas* (kahl-day-ron-NEES-tahs). In an effort to ward off a military coup, Figueres abolished the Costa Rican army in December 1948. He replaced it with the Civil Guard, made up of approximately 1,500 men led by loyal officers from his own National Liberation Army. For added protection Figueres signed the Río Treaty, a regional pact for mutual defense in case of attack against a national government. The United States was also a party to the treaty.

A woman at a polling station in Guidos searching for her name on a list. During the emergency rule of José Figueres, women were given the right to vote.

THE 1949 CONSTITUTION The new constitution was adopted in 1949 by an elected constituent assembly. It was the ninth constitution since 1825 and continues to serve as the foundation for the Costa Rican government. In addition to separating the executive, legislative, and judicial powers of government, it also established the Supreme Electoral Tribunal that controls the electoral process and supervises the Civil Registry. It prohibits a permanent army and the formation of any political party with ties to an international movement, effectively outlawing any Communist party. The 1949 constitution includes the Social Guarantees established under Calderón.

DON PEPE On November 8, 1949, Figueres and the other members of the ruling junta handed the reins of government over to Ulate and the Legislative Assembly as promised. Figueres was later hailed as "the grandfather of modern Costa Rica." He was affectionately called Don Pepe by the Costa Rican populace (Pepe is a common nickname for José). In 1951 Figueres founded the National Liberation Party (PLN) and announced his candidacy for president in the 1953 elections. The PLN was founded with the support of the middle class, and included business and agricultural interests. Don Pepe was elected in a landslide victory and went on to preside over what became a controversial presidential term. Public spending soared as he increased the number of public employees, raised the minimum wage, and increased public expenditure on education and housing.

CONFLICTS WITH NICARAGUA Figueres and the controversial president of Nicaragua, Anastasio Somoza García, had a deep personal dislike of each other and often supported each other's opponents in exile. In January 1955 hundreds of well-armed *calderonistas* invaded Costa Rica from across the Nicaraguan border and captured the town of Quesada. Figueres sought

The 1949 constitution drawn up by Figueres abolished the military. He explained the move by drawing an analogy. If a family member were ill, he said, the doctor would make a house call. But after that person recovered, there was no need for the doctor to live with the family for the rest of his life.

help from the United States under the Río Treaty. The Organization of American States ordered both countries to disassociate themselves from insurgent military forces in each other's territories. The two governments signed a formal treaty of friendship in December 1956, but border conflicts continued to flare up occasionally. Figueres was voted out of office in 1957 in favor of the Republican Party (PR), which carried on the *calderonista* legacy. The new president was unable to lower the large national debt, however, and the PLN recaptured power in the 1962 elections. This pattern was repeated over the next several elections, as the PLN alternately won and lost the presidency.

POLITICAL AND ECONOMIC CRISES The 1980s were characterized by political and military conflicts throughout the region. The U.S. Central Intelligence Agency established a base in Costa Rica from which to attack Sandinistas in Nicaragua despite opposition from the U.S. Congress. Many Nicaraguans sought refuge from the violence in Costa Rica, which added to tensions between Costa Ricans and Nicaraguans. The Costa Rican government also faced rising opposition at home. Once again the PLN's opponent was unable to reduce the external debt, and the PLN was voted back into power in the 1982 elections. By imposing austerity measures, the administration was able to pull the country out of the worst of its economic crisis. The PLN was reelected in 1986, installing Oscar Arias Sánchez as president.

A NOBEL PRESIDENT Arias found himself obliged to prolong many of the austerity measures of the previous administration in order to revive the economy. He also helped to bring an end to the regional political crisis. After nearly a decade of warfare in Nicaragua and El Salvador, Arias drafted

Sadinistas are members of a left-wing political party that are named after their leader and founder, Augusto César Sandino. The party overthrew the rule of the Somoza in 1979 and ruled Nicaragua for about 11 years. During this time, they established democratic elections and a national constitution.

a regional peace accord that proposed to end hostilities and to bring democracy to the war-torn countries. The five Central American presidents signed the accord on August 7, 1987. The Arias plan succeeded where other attempts had failed, largely because it was designed and agreed upon by the Central American governments themselves. President Arias was awarded the Nobel Peace Prize in 1987 for his role in the peace process.

Nonetheless, protests by labor unions and public employees mounted again during the late 1980s. The PLN lost the presidential and legislative elections in 1990, yielding power to Rafael Angel Calderón Fournier, who represented the Social Christian Unity Party (PUSC). Public dissatisfaction with the continued economic austerity measures helped the PLN to regain the presidency in 1994, represented by José María Figueres Olsen, the son of Don Pepe Figueres. The PLN did not win a majority in the Legislative Assembly though. Although the presidency subsequently went to the PUSC, in 2006 Arias was installed as president for the PLN for a second term.

Current president Oscar Arias Sánchez, who was reelected in 2006.

CORRUPTION SCANDAL

In 2004 three former presidents, José Maria Figueres, Rafael Angel Calderón Fournier, and Miguel Angel Rodriguez, were charged with fraud and corruption, damaging Costa Rica's democratic reputation. While Calderón and Rodríguez were subsequently arrested, Figueres, who is living in Spain, refuses to return to his country to face the charges.

GOVERNMENT

AS THE OLDEST DEMOCRATIC REPUBLIC in the region, Costa Rica is characterized by regular and fair elections, a literate and politically active population, and the abolition of its military. Every four years, on the first Sunday in February, Costa Ricans elect their president, vice presidents, members of the Legislative Assembly, and local members of the municipal councils. Citizens over the age of 18 are eligible to vote.

Above: **An election-day street rally.**

Opposite: **Costa Rica's national coat of arms. The seven stars represent Costa Rica's seven provinces, and the three volcanoes symbolize its mountain ranges. The merchant ships on the Pacific Ocean and the Caribbean Sea signify Costa Rica's cultural and economic exchanges with the rest of the world.**

NATIONAL GOVERNMENT

Costa Rica's national government is divided into three branches: executive, legislative, and judicial. There is also the Supreme Electoral Tribunal, which is almost a fourth branch in that it functions as a completely independent part of the government. Prior to the 1940s the Costa Rican government tried to limit its role in the economy. Since the presidency of Rafael Angel Calderón Guardia in the early 1940s, however, the government has intervened in the economy to the extent that its leaders have considered necessary in order to provide social benefits to the citizens. The government's hand in the economy is felt through its system of nationalized banking, petroleum refineries, and utilities. Social welfare priorities include public education and health and public assistance programs. Thus, in 1990 the United Nations declared Costa Rica to have the best human development index among underdeveloped countries. By 1992 Costa Rica was removed from the list of underdeveloped countries.

THE CONSTITUTION The modern republic is founded upon the 1949 constitution, which prohibits the president and legislators from being elected to more than one term in succession. It guarantees political rights for women and the right to a minimum wage for all citizens.

EXECUTIVE BRANCH The president heads the executive branch, and is assisted by two vice presidents, appointed cabinet ministers, and the Council of Government. The presidential candidate must receive at least 40 percent of the vote to win the election, after which he or she serves in office for four years. The duties of the president include appointing cabinet ministers, representing the country in official acts, and commanding the public security forces. In 1969 a constitutional amendment prohibited the president from serving more than once in a lifetime. In 2003, however, this was overturned, and now second presidential terms are allowed.

LEGISLATIVE BRANCH Costa Rica has a unicameral Legislative Assembly composed of 57 members. Deputies are elected for four-year terms, which may not be repeated successively. A deputy must be a Costa Rican citizen, either by birth or after 10 years of naturalization, and must be at least 21 years old. The 1949 constitution awards the primary share of power to the Legislative Assembly. This branch holds the exclusive powers to enact or repeal laws, approve the national

The debates of the Legislative Assembly are held in its modern legislature hall and are open to the public.

budget, levy taxes, and authorize the president to declare a national state of emergency. The Legislative Assembly may approve or reject international treaties and loans, appoint magistrates of the Supreme Court of Justice, and form new courts.

JUDICIAL BRANCH The Supreme Court of Justice rules over the country's judicial system and is divided into three chambers. The first chamber deals with appeals against administrative, civil, and commercial judgments made by the lower courts. The second chamber considers appeals against lower-court judgments on family issues, conflicts of jurisdiction between judicial and administrative authorities, and other matters. The third chamber considers criminal appeals, claims of injury and libel, and other matters relating to the criminal justice system.

President Arias posing with the cabinet ministers in San José.

ELECTORAL TRIBUNAL The Supreme Electoral Tribunal calls for the country's elections and controls the electoral process. It also supervises the Civil Registry, which issues identity cards, draws up voter lists, and records births, deaths, marriages, and naturalization. The Supreme Court of Justice appoints magistrates to the tribunal through a two-thirds vote, at staggered intervals so that the body always has a mixture of freshness and maturity.

The Costa Rican Mounted Police are a proud unit.

Costa Ricans resent any attempt by foreign powers to dominate them. During the regional political crisis of the 1980s, Costa Rica withstood pressures to follow the United States in its war against Nicaragua, despite U.S. sanctions on economic aid and diplomatic relations.

LOCAL GOVERNMENT

Costa Rica is divided administratively into provinces, cantons, and districts. There are seven provinces, but these have little administrative power. Rather, they serve primarily to partition the country into judicial and electoral jurisdictions. The president appoints governors to oversee the provinces, but their responsibilities are limited.

SECURITY FORCES

Costa Rica prides itself on having no standing military. In fact, its citizens grow indignant at the slightest hint of militarism. Even at the height of regional political instability in the 1980s, Costa Ricans strongly opposed any response that included increased national militarism. Instead, they take pride in their country's image as an oasis of tranquility. The enforcement of law and order rests on the police, and on air and naval communications, drug control, and intelligence units.

POLITICAL PARTIES

Until the 1940s political parties were formed primarily around the personal political ambitions of a single candidate. After the 1948 civil war the National Liberation Party (PLN) emerged as a party that attempted to represent a well-defined political platform. Nevertheless, the PLN continued to be identified with its founder, José Figueres, until his death in 1990, after which his son, José María Figueres, picked up the banner and announced immediately that he was running for president.

The Social Christian Unity Party is a coalition of four major groups: the Republican Calderonista Party, Democratic Renovation Party, Popular Unity Party, and Christian Democratic Party. For many years it was the strongest opposition party, alternating in power with the PLN since 1948, under different names and in various combinations. In 2000, though, the Citizen's Action Party (PAC) was formed and quickly became a strong presidential election contender. In the 2006 elections PAC leader Ottón Solis narrowly missed out on victory by fewer than 20,000 votes.

Nobel Peace Prize winner (1987) and president (1986–90, 2006–) Oscar Arias Sanchez, seen here with Pope Benedict XVI at the Vatican.

ECONOMY

AMONG ITS CENTRAL AMERICAN neighbors, Costa Rica has the largest per capita income and the highest standard of living. In 2005 the gross domestic product (GDP) was measured at $19.4 billion, roughly equivalent to $4,800 per person. This reflected a rise in the GDP of 4 percent over the previous year. Costa Rica and her neighbors support a free trade agreement with the United States called the Central America Free Trade Agreement (CAFTA). Under CAFTA, imports and exports to and from the United States will eventually become tariff free and American companies in Central America will be treated like local companies. The hope of the CAFTA is to bring about economic growth and stability for countries like Costa Rica.

Nevertheless, Costa Rica has been weathering an economic crisis for many years. One-tenth of the population still lives in absolute poverty, and inflation has fluctuated between 10 and 30 percent over the past two decades. While Costa Rica is relatively well off in comparison with other countries in the region, its prospects for economic growth remain hindered by its large foreign debt, equivalent to about one-quarter of the GDP.

Above: **Banco Nacional de Costa Rica in San José.**

Opposite: **Coffee is one of Costa Rica's top exports. Here, freshly harvested coffee fruit is packed in baskets before being taken away for processing.**

43

ECONOMIC UPS AND DOWNS

For nearly two decades Costa Rica suffered from economic constraints, which severely compromised efforts to maintain a strong system of social benefits. The national debt increased year after year to pay for social welfare programs. A shortfall in revenues was caused in part by a sharp decline in international coffee prices and exports. By 1981 the country's foreign debt had risen to $3 billion, and Costa Rica's total debt per person was the fourth highest in the world. Inflation was more than 50 percent, and unemployment had soared to nearly 10 percent.

In September 1981 the government was so far behind in interest payments on its foreign debt that it announced it was going to stop servicing the debt and requested that payments be rescheduled. Costa Rica thus became the first underdeveloped country to suspend debt payments, although a wave of such actions followed during the worldwide economic recession of the early 1980s. The International Monetary Fund (IMF), the World Bank, and the U.S. Agency for International Development agreed to lend Costa Rica money to meet its most pressing financial needs and to make up for revenue loss caused by declining coffee exports. They did this because the various organizations were anxious to avert any political consequences that might befall the only stable democracy in an otherwise volatile region.

They stipulated several conditions, including the requirement that the government devalue the Costa Rican currency, reduce public spending, lift price controls on gasoline and public utility charges, privatize several state agencies, and reform the tax system to improve methods of collection. By the early 1990s Costa Rica seemed to have resumed a slow economic recovery. The rate of increase in per capita income rose from 1 percent in 1990 to 7.7 percent by 1992. Nonetheless, from 2000 to 2004 the rate of increase dropped to around 1 percent before regaining significant ground in 2005.

A banana-sorting plant near Cahuita on the Caribbean coast.

EXPORTS

As in many less-developed countries, Costa Rica relies heavily on its exports for economic development. Bananas, coffee, sugar, and livestock constitute the bulk of traditional exports. Costa Rica is the second largest exporter of bananas in the world, after Ecuador. Banana exports continue to contribute most to export earnings.

Nontraditional agricultural export products (export crops or products introduced into a region where they have not been grown or harvested before) have also risen tremendously during the past couple of decades. These exports include flowers, ornamental plants and foliage, fresh and frozen fish, shrimp, melons, macadamia nuts, and pineapples. In fact, pineapple production has surpassed that of coffee as the country's second largest agricultural export. Unfortunately for Costa Rican farmers, most of the nontraditional export trade, with the exception of fish, is controlled by foreign-owned companies that have better access to technology and marketing strategies and take most of the profit. Other major crops include cocoa, cotton, and hemp.

PRIMARY OCCUPATIONS AND INDUSTRIES

Agriculture and livestock are a major part of Costa Rica's economy, but the economic profile is changing. In the 1950s, 50 percent of the labor force worked in agriculture, turning out 95 percent of total exports. Industry contributed only 13 percent of the gross domestic product. With membership in the Central American Common Market, however, Costa Rica has increased its industrial production, and, with government assistance in high-tech industries, more people are seeking jobs in the urban areas. The sectors of industry, information technology, and tourism are gaining increasing dominance in the economy.

AGRICULTURE Farmers are able to produce a wide variety of crops because of the range of climates in the country. Besides export crops, they also cultivate crops for domestic consumption. These include beans, corn, plantains, potatoes, rice, sorghum (a grain similar to corn), onions, and African palms, from which they derive palm oil. Farmers also raise livestock for the domestic market, including cattle, pigs, horses, mules, sheep, goats, and chickens.

Oil palm harvest on the Pacific coast. Oil comes from both its fruit and the fruit seeds.

FORESTRY The forests are generally viewed as obstacles to progress, and timber is often burned or left to rot. There is no formal system of reforestation, and most developers and landless peasants do not see

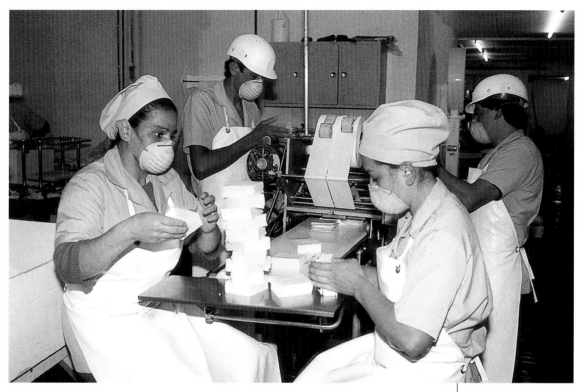

the need for such a program. Despite this bleak picture, Costa Rica is internationally renowned for its efforts to conserve its natural environment. The government has set aside a quarter of the land area for national parks, forest reserves, indigenous reservations, and wildlife refuges. The legislature has also passed laws to protect Costa Rica's land, water, and forests—although the laws are often disregarded by developers.

INDUSTRY Costa Rica produces a wide variety of light manufactured goods. While food, beverages, and tobacco have traditionally been the main manufacturing activities, electronics, pharmaceuticals, and software development have become key industries in recent years. Other manufactured goods include rubber, plastics, chemicals, textiles, adhesives, cosmetics, bricks and cement, fertilizer, and wood products.

Mining and manufacturing together contributed about 22 percent of the GDP in 2004. Mining consists primarily of the extraction of nonmetallic minerals such as limestone, sand, salt, and clay. Gold and silver are also mined

A cheese factory in Monteverde. Modern manufacturing of cheese began in the early 20th century and the sector expanded rapidly in the 1960s.

in small amounts. Costa Ricans have been searching for petroleum for more than a century, but deposits have shown little economic potential. Intensified interest by international firms in conducting oil exploration on Costa Rican soil prompted the government in 2002 to take a firm environmental stand and prohibit all oil exploration. An oil pipeline does, however, carry imported crude oil to a refinery at Moín where the oil is redistributed to the highlands and other regions of Costa Rica.

Hydroelectric power provides the primary source of electrical energy. With its abundant rainfall and favorable terrain, Costa Rica has enormous hydroelectric potential, and about a dozen hydroelectric plants have been built on various rivers. Other energy sources include diesel and gas turbine generation for electricity, as well as the burning of wood, charcoal, and bagasse (vegetable waste, primarily from sugarcane).

A hydroelectric dam on the Reventazón River.

TOURISM With its abundance of natural beauty, ecotourism in Costa Rica is booming. Over the past few years, the number of visitors has increased by about 20 percent a year, reaching 1.5 million visitors in 2005. Indeed, tourism has become one of the country's primary sources of revenue, surpassing the export earnings of both bananas and coffee combined.

SERVICES The services sector is the largest area of the economy, employing roughly 60 percent of the labor force and generating 61 percent of the country's GDP. Services include social, financial, communal, and personal services in occupational areas such as transportation, health care, restaurants and hotels, communications, real estate, and insurance.

TRANSPORTATION AND COMMUNICATIONS

Improved transportation and communications have linked all parts of the country and opened it up tremendously during the last few decades. The Meseta Central, or Central Valley, serves as the hub of the transportation system. The major highways and railroads extend from there to the Pacific and Caribbean lowlands. Transportation systems include railroads, a domestic air service, inland waterways, and roads for the increased number of cars and buses. The Pan-American Highway runs the length of the country, from the Nicaraguan border to Panama. Inland waterways act as important conduits for communication, cargo, and passengers in the north and northeastern parts of the country. Two important routes are the San Carlos and Sarapiquí rivers, both of which flow northward through the plains.

Communication systems in Costa Rica include the telegraph, telephone, radio, television, the Internet, newspapers, and several periodicals. In 2004 about 90 percent of households had a television, and about one in every three people owned a telephone or mobile phone.

The streets of San José are often crowded with people and traffic. In the last several decades, Costa Rica's government has built highways and improved roads throughout the country.

49

ENVIRONMENT

COSTA RICA'S DIVERSE NATURAL LANDSCAPE attracts people from all over the world who come to marvel at its astonishing beauty. Within Costa Rica itself, however, there is a fair amount of discontent with the government regarding its environmental efforts.

The Nature Conservancy, an international organization whose mission it is to preserve flora and fauna by protecting their habitats, conducted a survey among Costa Ricans in 2005. The survey revealed that the majority of Costa Ricans are as concerned about serious environmental problems such as air and water pollution as they are about crime rates and public health services. While the government seems to be doing many things right, having achieved one of the best conservation records in the world, it still has some way to go in other areas that affect the quality of life for average Costa Ricans.

Above: **The Nature Conservancy hopes to protect animals such as the cougar from extinction by protecting their natural habitats.**

Opposite: Waterfalls like this can be found on the slopes of Volcán Arenal.

DEFORESTATION

With Costa Rica's world-class achievements in conservation, it might be surprising to learn that by the 1990s much of the country had been deforested. In fact, Costa Rica has one of the worst deforestation rates in Central America, with forests being felled at an alarming rate of more than 193 square miles (500 square km) a month. Once densely covered, much of the terrain has been cleared for large-scale commercial agricultural developments, in particular, for coffee and banana plantations and cattle pastures. In addition, the growing population continually exerts pressure on the government to clear land for human habitation.

51

Costa Rica complies with many environmental treaties, including the Convention of Biological Diversity, the United Nations Framework Convention on Climate Change, the Endangered Species Convention, and the Convention on Marine Dumping, to name a few.

Deforestation has resulted in many animal and plant species becoming endangered. With no forest cover to protect the land, the soil is exposed to the sun and the rain, leaving it thin, dry, and easily washed away. Natural water sources such as rivers and streams are also affected, becoming more prone to flooding or drying up.

To stem the rate of deforestation, the government has initiated some innovative forest protection programs to promote sustainable development. One such program involves a forest management plan for landowners, entitling them to payment for every acre of forest protected. The government has also tried to promote reforestation through tax incentives. While deforestation rates have dropped, the remaining forests are still threatened by illegal logging. In sharp contrast to 85 percent of forest cover in 1940, today only about 50 percent of the land remains forested, two-thirds of which are protected.

NATIONAL PARKS AND CONSERVATION

In 1970 Costa Rica established its greatly admired national park system, covering all of the country's major ecosystems and habitats. There are

TRADING FORESTS FOR GREENHOUSE GASES

At a UN summit on climate change in 2005, Costa Rica was part of a coalition of ten developing countries that successfully proposed a deal for wealthy nations to compensate poor nations for tropical rain forest conservation. The deal is based on the preservation of forests in developing countries as a counter to greenhouse gas emissions in wealthy countries prospering from urbanization. Deforestation is one of the major contributors to global warming, accounting for about one-quarter of greenhouse gas emissions, or about two billion tons of carbon per year. It is hoped that slowing deforestation will help slow climate change.

currently 26 national parks managed by the Ministry of Environment and Energy (MINAE). It is responsible for 161 protected areas. Apart from the national parks, these include biological reserves, forest reserves, wildlife refuges, wetlands, mangroves, and marine areas. Together, the protected areas cover approximately one-quarter of Costa Rica and provide a safe haven for about 75 percent of the country's species of flora and fauna.

In 1998 MINAE established 11 regional conservation areas, which are known as Sistema Nacional de Areas de Conservación (National System of Conservation Areas), or SINAC. As part of this system, several parks, private conservation areas, and other protected zones have been joined together and now encompass complete and unique ecosystems. The aim is to provide larger areas in which wildlife can migrate and move around. The conservation areas are Arenal Huetar Norte, Arenal Tilarán, Caribbean La Amistad, Pacific La Amistad, Central Volcanic Cordillera, Central Pacific, Guanacaste, Osa, Tempisque, Tortuguero, and Cocos Island Marine.

Costa Rica also has many conservation groups that have taken on various roles and responsibilities, from managing private nature reserves to setting up forest management projects. Efforts have also been made to involve local communities by integrating their livelihoods into the day-to-day operation of the national park system. The purpose of this is to teach locals that it is possible to earn a living by preserving rather than destroying the environment.

Despite Costa Rica's numerous national parks and efforts at conservation, deforestation still remains a problem and a threat.

Costa Rica is home to three UNESCO World Heritage Sites: Guanacaste Conservation Area, Cocos Island, and La Amistad International Park.

In 1996 Costa Rica banned the use of leaded gasoline. In addition, all motor vehicles must pass an annual emissions inspection and imported cars must be equipped with catalytic converters.

WASTE MANAGEMENT

While Costa Rica's conservation system is world class, its water and waste management systems are still lacking. Almost all Costa Ricans have access to a water supply source. However, while the water supply in San José is filtered and chlorinated, the same cannot be said for the water outside the capital. There is also no sewage treatment facility in any city in Costa Rica, including San José. Almost half of the country's municipalities throw their refuse onto open dumps. Costa Rica is not alone in this respect, as only about 2 percent of raw sewage is treated across the whole of Central America.

Some areas in particular are experiencing the disastrous consequences of the lack of a decent sewage system. Practically all of the sewage from the highly populated Central Valley is pumped untreated into the Tarcoles River. The town of Tarcoles on the Pacific Coast is now facing a desperate situation. Once a popular destination for tourists, it is now given a wide berth, as the river running through it reeks and bubbles with sewage.

In light of this, the government has plans to clean the river by building a wastewater treatment plant in San José. It will have the capacity to

THE CHALLENGE OF ECOTOURISM

Ecotourism is the practice of visiting natural habitats or attractions with as little impact to the environment as possible. Ecotourism in Costa Rica is a booming business. On the surface, that appears to be a good thing. Attracting more visitors to the parks means more revenue and more job opportunities. There are concerns in some quarters, however, that Costa Rica's ecotourism drive could actually end up damaging the ecology, as developers clear land to construct new hotels and facilities that cater to growing waves of tourists. The challenge for the government is to balance the demands of the ecotourism industry with long-term conservation needs.

handle the sewage generated by about 65 percent of the Central Valley population and will be the first of its size in the region. Residents along the river and at the Tarcoles seaside will have to wait a while longer for things to improve, however, as the first stage of construction is not expected to be completed until around 2017.

MARINE POLLUTION

Waste and pollutants from urban centers in Costa Rica flow into its rivers and into the ocean, which has had a devastating effect on marine life. This can be seen along the shorelines and coral reefs, and in the death of marine

The lack of proper waste management facilities and education in protecting water sources in Costa Rica has led to many rivers becoming clogged with sewage and pollution, rendering the water unpotable.

WATER FOR LIFE

In the early 1990s local residents of Puerto Viejo, a village near the Caribbean coast, ran out of potable water. The river water that they were accustomed to drinking had become polluted with sewage and garbage (*as pictured here*). Their search for clean water elsewhere prompted a research biologist at the Universidad Nacional Autonoma de Costa Rica, Dr. Claudia Charpentier, who had been studying the waterways in that area, to include community outreach in her project. She developed the Water for Life program, an environmental education program focused on water quality and quantity in the lowlands of Costa Rica. To this day graduate students, educators, and local community leaders play an active role in developing teaching materials to help villagers understand the connection between the environment, human activities, and clean drinking water. The aim is to empower them with the knowledge of how to safeguard their local water sources.

As a result of severe water pollution, marine life in the seas and in the rivers flowing into them have suffered.

life such as fish, turtles, and dolphins. The Caribbean shorelines are also clogged with soil deposits washed into the waterways as a result of deforestation and natural disasters. In addition, the indiscriminate dumping of industrial waste from ships at sea damages the fragile marine ecosystem.

AGRICULTURAL IMPACT

While Costa Rica's main traditional agricultural products—bananas and coffee—have provided a foundation for economic growth, the environment has paid a price. For example, large tracts of land have been deforested in order to make way for banana plantations. Furthermore, today's cultivation is also marked by the high use of pesticides and fertilizers. In fact, Costa Rica has one of the highest rates of pesticide use, more than twice the average used in other parts of the region. Apart from displacing whole communities of wildlife and destroying the biodiversity of flora and fauna, the clearing of forest cover and intense use of pesticides have contaminated much of the soil and reduced it to silt, which gets washed away by the rain into nearby streams and rivers.

Banana plantations also generate vast amounts of waste—double the volume of bananas produced. There are generally two types of waste—biodegradable (organic) and nonbiodegradable. Organic waste consists of the shoots, leaves, flowers, and other parts of the banana plant, which are either added back to the soil or thrown into large open-air dumps. Because these plant parts are very fibrous, they may decompose very slowly. As they are often not treated, the risk of bacterial build-up is high, and leaching from the waste may seep into underground water sources.

Nonbiodegradable waste includes the plastic bags, containers, and string used to wrap or pack the bananas. Plastic bags are commonly used during the growing period to protect the fruit from insects, and the bags are often impregnated with an insecticide. Although there are laws on pollution control regarding proper treatment of waste, they are not strictly adhered to. While some plantations burn or recycle these bags after use, others throw them into open dumps. They are even found floating in rivers or the sea, polluting the water and affecting river and marine life.

In the case of coffee, the story is much the same. Waste products are dumped into waterways, which is hazardous because the coffee bean contains contaminants that can destroy fauna and harm people. In the 1970s a new species of coffee plant, called the sun coffee plant, was introduced. It requires much more sunlight and results in a bigger loss of trees and soil erosion. The fruit of the coffee tree is called a cherry. Another environmental problem lies in the process of separating the ripe cherry pulp from its seeds—the coffee beans. After fermenting in a water tank for a day, the pulp is separated from the beans, which are set out in the sun to dry. The sugared water from the pulp drains into rivers, starving aquatic life of oxygen and depleting it.

A worker at a banana plantation cutting off the fibrous stalks of bananas before processing them.

COSTA RICANS

COSTA RICANS CALL THEMSELVES "TICOS" (TEE-kohs)—a nickname that connotes their national pride and sense of uniqueness. They identify themselves first as Costa Ricans and as Latin Americans or Central Americans almost as an afterthought. They explain certain actions or behavior by saying, "We Ticos are like that," and proudly speak of their "idiosyncrasy" or "national reality," which they perceive to be unique.

In terms of its culture and ethnic composition, Costa Rica is relatively homogenous. For this reason Ticos have traditionally prided themselves on being "whiter" than other Central Americans, and associated their ethnic homogeneity with their tradition of democracy, political stability, and high level of literacy.

Costa Rica has long served as a sanctuary for exiles from other countries—from Central American and Eastern European refugees escaping political persecution to drug lords and arms traffickers fleeing criminal prosecution.

ETHNIC GROUPS

Given the relatively small indigenous population at the time of the Spanish conquest, most indigenous people were either quickly absorbed into the Hispanic population or marginalized in isolated areas. The term mestizo was used to distinguish those of mixed indigenous and European ancestry for only a short while. It was not long before most mestizos called themselves "white."

Approximately 94 percent of the 4 million population is white or mestizo. About 3 percent of the Costa Rican populace is black, while

Above: **Some Costa Ricans sitting by the road for a rest.**

Opposite: **A Costa Rican man enjoying fresh coconut juice after a morning of hard work.**

1 percent is Chinese and another 1 percent is of indigenous origin. Ethnic conflict is limited in Costa Rica, perhaps because Ticos tend to shun conflict or, more likely, because minorities are such a small percentage of the population. Most mestizos are descended from the Spanish and the Chorotega Indians. They speak a slightly different Spanish dialect from the rest of the highland population. Within this homogenous society, however, certain cultural traditions can be distinguished. In addition to the indigenous and the Spanish-American traditions, one can also observe distinct cultural traditions.

INDIGENOUS Besides those with mixed indigenous and European ancestry, the remaining indigenous population is very small in relation to the rest of the Costa Rican population. The people prefer to be called *indígenas* (een-DEE-hay-nahs) rather than Indians or *indios* (EEN-dyos). There are eight ethnic groups, totaling about 60,000 people. Most live near the southern border and work as subsistence farmers.

The largest indigenous group is the Talamanca, a name given to the Bribri and Cabécar peoples who live

Bribri Indians in the Talamanca region, weaving a basket.

a rather isolated existence on either side of the Cordillera de Talamanca. Together they make up roughly two-thirds of the total indigenous population. Their pre-Columbian ancestors escaped to this region after the Spanish conquest. The Boruca group, numbering between 1,500 and 2,000, forms the second-largest indigenous population, which lives primarily within three villages in the southwest. Most of them are Spanish speaking.

In the 1960s the Legislative Assembly created the National Commission of Indian Affairs (CONAI) to improve the social, economic, and cultural situations of the indigenous people and to urge that they be granted the rights and guarantees of full citizenship. Regrettably, this has not yet fully happened. In 1976 the government set aside five land areas for the indigenous population. Now there are 22 Indian reservations. Nonindigenous persons are not allowed to rent, lease, or buy that land. Enforcement of these restrictions in the protected areas has been shaky, however.

BLACKS In contrast to many African-American populations in the Western hemisphere, Costa Rica's black citizens are not descended from slaves. In fact, an 1862 law prohibited the immigration of both blacks and Asians. When this prohibition was lifted in the late 1800s, many blacks emigrated from Jamaica to work on the Costa Rican railroad project. After the project was completed, many stayed for jobs on the banana plantations.

Costa Rica's black minority group is located mainly on the Caribbean coast. They planted the coconut trees that now line the beaches.

By the mid-1920s white Costa Ricans from the Meseta Central began to resent the black banana workers. They charged that the blacks got better jobs in supervisory and clerical positions because they could speak English to the North American supervisors. The whites endeavored to place restrictions on the movements and rights of blacks. Because the blacks were never allowed to own land, white highlanders found it easy to evict them from

Pedestrians on Avenida Central in San José. Although class differences exist, they are not as divisive as in other countries in the region.

the farms they had created in the Caribbean lowlands. Laws prevented their migrating out of the Caribbean lowlands, and by the 1930s most blacks had been reduced to poverty. Many immigrated to Panama or the United States in search of better opportunities. They were finally given full citizenship rights after the 1948 revolution. Black Ticos still tend to be concentrated in the Caribbean coast, however, and they have had a notable influence on the language, culture, and cuisine of Limón province.

CHINESE More than 600 Chinese laborers came to Costa Rica in 1873 after the prohibition against Asian immigration was lifted briefly to admit railroad workers. The contracts of these Chinese laborers included a provision that they would be sent home as soon as construction was completed. They were paid one-fifth of the normal wage and forced to live and work under miserable conditions. Rather than being returned to China, many of those who survived were sold into household service in the homes of hidalgos.

Today the Chinese population, known as *chinos* (CHEE-nohs), constitutes an important part of Costa Rican society. The first-generation immigrants tended to isolate themselves within their own neighborhoods. Their children, on the other hand, have integrated into the wider community with little difficulty or prejudice. The Chinese tend to distinguish themselves as successful businesspeople, often owning most of the retail stores, restaurants, cinemas, hotels, and bars in some smaller towns.

SOCIAL HIERARCHY

Since Costa Rica is relatively homogeneous in terms of ethnicity and culture, the main divisions within the society are among the social classes and between rural and urban residents. Most Ticos who possess any measure of power, wealth, or status are concentrated in the urban areas of the Meseta Central—especially in San José.

Ironically, most Ticos denigrate manual labor, in spite of the fact that they pride themselves on their democratic foundations and cherish the national myth of the yeoman farmer. They may respect the campesinos, or peasants, as hard workers, but look down on them for being manual laborers.

UPPER CLASS Members of the middle class may move into the upper class through marriage, by obtaining a professional degree, or by entering politics. The upper class constitutes about 5 percent of the population and consists of two levels: the principal families and the newly rich. The principal families, also called *la societal* (soh-see-eh-TAL) or the society,

Various elements can be distinguished within the middle class. Mingled among the broad definitions of upper and lower middle class is the conventional middle class, consisting of the bureaucracy and salaried employees.

DISTRIBUTION OF WEALTH

Although they consider it crass to think only of money, most Costa Ricans still perceive wealth as the primary determinant of class position, along with education and occupation. Education is highly valued as the surest route to upward mobility. The government facilitates social and economic opportunity by providing education, pensions, and free health care to its citizens. Nevertheless, inequities in income do exist and recent surveys indicate that the gap between rich and poor may be widening. In 2004 the top 20 percent of society received approximately 52 percent of the national income, while the bottom 20 percent got only 4.6 percent of total income.

Many peasants feel that economic and social success comes from a combination of hard work and good luck. It is believed, for example, that good luck allows a person to be born rich so that they can pursue education and power.

Ticos in the Meseta Central do not usually appear in public wearing shorts, which is considered as low-class attire.

correspond to the hidalgos of the colonial era. They are descended from the early gentry and continue to play a strong role in politics.

MIDDLE CLASS Approximately 25 percent of the population form the middle class in Costa Rica. Many were children who came from working-class backgrounds but managed to move into the middle class through education. The growth of the public sector has also enabled many people to move into the middle class as bureaucrats. The upper middle class consists of professionals such as doctors, lawyers, and engineers; less wealthy industrialists and merchants; and large landowners without secondary enterprises. They tend to be well educated and may mix with members of the upper class in some social contexts. The lower middle class, on the other hand, consists of white-collar workers, small business owners, and low-salaried professionals such as nurses.

LOWER URBAN CLASS This group can be divided into two subgroups, the working class and the marginals. Industrial development in the 20th century produced a large urban working class, which today forms approximately 50 percent of the population. The working class maintains a reasonably steady income, earning salaries above the minimum wage. The marginals often live below the poverty line. This group includes street vendors, unskilled workers, and domestic servants.

PEASANTRY The campesinos, or peasants, far from disdaining manual labor, place a high value on hard physical work. In fact, many campesinos regard office work and most urban occupations as overpaid and not real work at all. In addition to hard work, peasants generally value thriftiness and simple living, as opposed to the conspicuous consumption often seen among status-seeking urbanites.

DRESS

Costa Ricans value physical appearance highly; even the poorest Ticos strive to present a well-groomed and neat appearance in everyday life. They may skimp on food or other necessities in order to dress stylishly and thus appear as successful as possible. Some may say that clothing is the cheapest status symbol they can buy, since it is easier to obtain than a nice house or luxury car.

Although they always dress neatly, the people do not necessarily always dress formally. Men from the upper and middle classes often put aside their suit coats in favor of short-sleeved shirts with a tie, or even a sport shirt. Young people dress more casually and often wear T-shirts and jeans.

Most teenagers prefer to dress in American-style casual clothes.

LIFESTYLE

THE MOST-PRIZED CULTURAL VALUES of Costa Ricans are family, a formal education, democracy, peace, and individual liberty. On an individual level, people place great value on the extended family, which for most Ticos provides the most important source of social contact. On the national level, Costa Ricans pride themselves on their tradition of democracy, reflected in the belief that Costa Rica, albeit small, is a sovereign and independent nation.

SOCIAL INTERACTIONS

Peace is a central value for Costa Ricans, both on a political and personal level. Ticos prefer moderation and compromise over conflict with other people. Rather than committing themselves to a specific position, they are much more likely to hold their opinions in reserve by saying, "who knows?" or "perhaps." This reflects their desire for *quedar bien* (kay-DAR bee-EN), or getting along. The saying "Each in his own house and God in all," expresses the same inclination toward harmonious coexistence.

QUEDAR BIEN This attitude governs everyday relations between Ticos. It reflects their wish to leave a good impression and to maintain their dignity. It can assume extreme social proportions, however, since the desire for *quedar bien* often leads people to say things they do not mean or to make promises they do not intend to keep. The immediate cost of saying "no" is thus avoided in favor of a smiling assent, leaving the rejection for a later time. This does not mean that Ticos try to be

Above: **A woman at a fruit stall. Costa Ricans try to treat everyone they encounter with respect. They may be friendly but also maintain a sense of dignity and are careful not to offend one another.**

Opposite: **Girls in the town of Puerto Viejo. Life in towns like this is quiet. Many people get around on foot or by bicycle.**

dishonorable; on the contrary, they simply hope that the moment of disagreeable truth will be indefinitely delayed. For example, promising to do something mañana, although literally signifying tomorrow, may mean that they will do it tomorrow, some day, or never. This common social maneuver of saying "yes, but no," helps to avoid friction and thus sustain *quedar bien*.

CHOTEO (cho-TAY-oh) Ticos also regard boasting of any kind as vulgar and antisocial. Regardless of social or economic status, they consider it important to act with humility, which enhances their dignity by

Many Costa Ricans say they prefer to remain casual acquaintances with people outside their family as this helps them to avoid problems such as becoming an object of gossip.

allowing them to preserve a positive image in front of others. Boasting or pretentiousness of any kind is likely to provoke *choteo*, or mockery.

Choteo can range from friendly irony to malicious sarcasm. It also acts as a form of social control, since people fear doing anything that would provoke gossip or ridicule. Although Ticos like to think of themselves as individualists, they are not necessarily nonconformists. Social interactions tend to be fairly conservative and highly defined by the values of coexistence and *quedar bien*. Ticos are quick to gossip about and criticize others but fear becoming the object of *choteo* themselves.

Ticos value their personal dignity so avidly that extreme forms of *choteo* can cause legal trouble. Under Costa Rican law it is illegal to defame someone's honor or impugn the memory of the deceased, since that dishonors the surviving family. Thus politicians must be careful not to attack their opponents on a personal level. On the other hand, Ticos tend to be extremely critical of themselves as individuals and as a society.

PERSONALISM Personal relations are very important in Costa Rican society. The honor and reputation of the individual and family are carefully protected because the individual depends on his image and personal connections to obtain employment, political advancement, and favors, and even to sidestep legal problems should they arise.

Ticos generally go out of their way to preserve one another's dignity in face-to-face interactions. They treat each other with formal greetings and flowing compliments. In this sense they are a very sociable people and have no problem striking up friendly conversations with strangers.

Although they avoid solitude, Costa Ricans greatly value their privacy. Their surface friendliness masks an inner reserve that often makes them wary of forming intimate friendships outside of their families.

Ticos are strongly oriented toward their own families, villages, and neighborhoods, almost to the exclusion of the larger society or world. They have a traditional saying: "There is no bread like that baked at home."

Men are expected to be brave and aggressive in their actions.

A Costa Rican adage describes the superiority of men by saying, "The rooster sings; the hen only cackles."

GENDER ROLES

The Costa Ricans' belief in the equality and dignity of all human beings does not necessarily translate into the gender roles they have defined for men and women. From early childhood, girls are taught and expected to be weaker, more emotional, and more vulnerable, and to show less intelligence than boys. Young boys are taught and expected to be more demanding and aggressive than girls and to shine in the classroom.

MACHISMO Men are expected to be macho and daring. They prove their masculinity, or machismo, by flirting with women, as well as through exploits such as bullfighting and auto racing—or simply by their behavior while driving through traffic. It is not unusual for men to hiss, whistle, or address *piropos* (pee-ROH-pohs), that is, catcalls, to women walking on the street.

Men and boys are taught from an early age to do as they please. Within the family, they generally do not share the responsibility for household chores, and any suggestion of so-called effeminate behavior is ridiculed. Things may be looking up, though, as today's middle-class men are more likely to help their wives around the house.

MARIANISMO (mah-ree-ahn-EES-moh) For girls, the concept of physical beauty is strongly emphasized. "Queen" contests, or beauty pageants, celebrate feminine beauty for girls and young women in almost every imaginable context. Advertising also perpetuates the sexually attractive feminine ideal. Females learn to receive compliments on their beauty from men and women alike.

Women are expected to serve their husbands and boyfriends, and are responsible for household chores. The feminine ideal of *marianismo* demands that women remain loyal, chaste, and submissive, even in the face of a husband's sexual infidelities. Although men are mostly perceived as superior, women are considered to be the stronger sex in moral and spiritual integrity. A woman's virtue is expressed through the sacrifice of her own pleasures for the well-being of her family. One of the highest compliments is for a wife to be described as self-sacrificing.

A Costa Rican woman's reputation and virtue must be protected, and she must carefully avoid becoming an object of gossip. Yet in spite of the social restrictions imposed on women, as many as 50 percent of children are born out of wedlock, and more than 40 percent of poor families are headed by a single mother. This may reflect the perpetual machismo attitude within Costa Rican culture. In response to this condition, the Law of Fatherhood was passed in 2001 outlining a father's legal obligation to support his children. The traditional role of women has been changing, however, and Costa Rican women are becoming better educated and more liberated. Increasing numbers of middle- and upper-class women are entering the professional, technical, and clerical workforces. Dating without chaperons is also more common than it used to be.

Costa Rican women perform their duties as mother to the best of their abilities and without complaints.

A park in San José.

URBAN AND RURAL SOCIETY

The contrast between urban and rural living is the basis of economic and social divisions. Most upper- and upper-middle-class people live in the urban areas concentrated in the Meseta Central, close to the capital. These areas are characterized by a higher number of motorized vehicles and a wider distribution of telephones and television sets.

Cities, towns, and most villages are divided into barrios, or neighborhoods. Most Ticos identify strongly with their own barrio, although the upper-class citizens might identify themselves as Costa Ricans or even as citizens of the world. The lower-income barrios tend to be more closely knit, since residents often rely on each other for mutual aid. With the deterioration of the economy in the 1980s and early 1990s, though, even those traditionally close barrio relationships have faded. People move around more, always seeking to improve their conditions, and crime rates, especially for robbery, have increased. In some wealthier urban neighborhoods, a watchman might be employed to protect the area.

Cities, towns, and villages in the highlands are usually laid out in a grid pattern, centered around a plaza with a fountain, colorful plants, benches, and a bandstand. The main government buildings and businesses are situated as closely as possible to the center of town. The larger towns have schools, restaurants, hotels, a bus station, a hospital, and a large covered marketplace.

Rural settlements, in contrast, are still characterized to some degree by a lack of streets, blocks, and sidewalks, and the absence of a municipal water supply, electricity, and other urban services. They have a central

An upper-class home in San José.

plaza that is usually no more than a grassy square used for soccer. There will usually be a school nearby, a *pulpería* (pool-pay-REE-ah) or general store, and a small church where a visiting priest will conduct Mass once or twice a month. In some places the same building serves as the school and church.

HOUSING The wealthier urban residents usually live in one- or two-story houses, with a low front porch and a well-kept lawn in front, enclosed by a fence and gate, and a patio courtyard in the middle of or behind the house. Most houses have iron grilles over their windows, and the owners may keep one or two guard dogs.

In contrast, poor urban residents often live in unpainted shacks or in deteriorated buildings that have been divided into crowded apartments. These makeshift dwellings make up the *auguries* (aw-GOO-ryes), or slums, of Costa Rican cities. The floors of the shanties may consist of packed dirt, wooden planks, or broken tiles. Lower-class urban workers fashion homes for themselves from these poor materials and keep them as neat and clean as conditions permit.

HEALTH AND WELFARE

Costa Rica has one of the highest standards of health care in Central America. The Ministry of Health emphasizes preventive measures to ensure a healthy population, including programs that provide potable water, prevent malnutrition, and immunize against diseases. Among its successes is the government-run Program for Rural Health, which extends a network of health units throughout the country to the most rural areas and works to prevent illness through preschool education and nutrition centers. In 2004 there was one doctor for every 582 residents and one hospital bed for about every 700 people. Although the health-care system is still not easily accessible in the more isolated areas of the country, life expectancy has risen to 74 years for males and 80 years for females. The infant mortality rate—10 deaths per 1,000 Costa Ricans in 2006—is also far below that of most Latin American countries.

Costa Rica has been recognized internationally for its declining rate of population growth. In 1960 the country showed a 4 percent annual rate of natural increase. By 1973 the rate of natural increase had dropped to 2.5 percent, one of the sharpest declines in the world. During this period the number of surviving children born to the average Costa Rican woman was reduced from 7.3 to 4.1 children. By 2006 the rate of natural increase had dropped to just 1.45 percent.

Alcohol use and abuse by young Costa Ricans is a growing problem. Drunkenness is discouraged, but the consumption of alcohol forms a

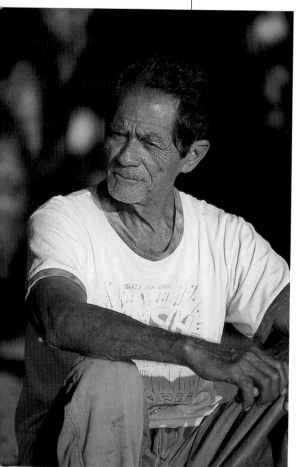

Costa Ricans enjoy a fairly high standard of health care, which is evidenced by a longer life expectancy, but problems such as obesity and alcoholism are on the rise.

large part of leisure activities. The culture of machismo exacerbates the problem, since refusal to drink may be viewed as effeminate. Some observers of Costa Rican society also feel that the rapid social, economic, and cultural changes of the past few decades have contributed to disorientation and instability within the culture, provoking a rise in both alcohol and drug abuse.

DAILY ROUTINE

The daily routine and diet of Ticos depends on their occupation and social

A family in Puntarenas relaxes at home.

class. The average urban Costa Rican men and children rise around five or six o'clock, and take a cold shower or bath. After dressing neatly, they present themselves at the breakfast table, where the women have prepared a simple meal of coffee, rice, and beans. They leave for work or school early and may return home for the midday meal. These days, fewer Ticos take the time to enjoy a midday siesta, or nap, before returning to work or school.

On the way home the husband may stop by a cantina, or bar, for an hour or so before returning home for dinner. He plays with his children before they have a light supper. After dinner, he may either stay at home watching television or listening to the radio or return to the cantina while his wife finishes the housework or sews. The older children either stay at home or go out with their friends. Most do not spend much time studying. On normal evenings, family members go to bed by 10 or 11 P.M.

LIFE CYCLE EVENTS

FAMILY Costa Ricans consider family to be the cornerstone of society. Their closest relationships are usually derived from within the family, and they spend much of their leisure time with their relatives. With the declining birth rate, large families are now less common. Couples often decide to have fewer children because they do not want to spread their resources too thinly. It is also not unusual for children to live with their parents until they marry.

Women from the lower class tend to be more confined to family relationships than middle- and upper-class women. Poor women work very hard from childhood onward, first helping their mothers, then managing the many heavy responsibilities of their own households.

Despite societal expectations of women, many Costa Rican children are actually born out of wedlock, and come from single-parent homes. Female-headed households are more common among the poor, where fathers abandon their families or the mothers do not sustain long-term relationships. In Costa Rica, living together in a free union without being married is recognized. Such relationships are most common among lower-income couples and in the lowland provinces.

Three generations share a small shack in a lower-class barrio. All-female households exist where the father has abandoned the family.

Although they lack the social prestige of married couples, men and women in free unions are seldom disparaged, although for women, it is an apparent contradiction of the feminine ideal of virtue and chastity. Women in such open relationships have the same legal rights as wives.

Children born out of wedlock, called *hijos naturales* (EE-hoes nah-tur-AHL-ays) or children of nature, are not stigmatized. In cases where their birth is the result of the mother's short-term affair with a man from the middle or upper class, the father will often provide for the support and education of the child. Many upper-class wives, socialized by the ethic of *marianismo*, tolerate this expense: "After all, it's not the fault of the child."

Many rural households are families with no menfolk, in which case the grandmother usually stays at home to care for the small children, while her daughter works to support the family. The grandmother, as the matriarch of the family, runs the household.

The father generally does not help with housework but often finds time to play with his children or take the family out.

BIRTH Costa Ricans love and cherish children. Women generally celebrate their first pregnancy and welcome one or two more babies. Most births occur in a hospital or health center, which has contributed to the decline in infant and maternal mortality rates. Parents still choose godparents (*padrinos*) for the baby, although the role of the godparent is no longer as important as in the past. Traditionally, godparents were expected to assume responsibility for the religious instruction of the godchild. In this manner, they also contribute to the child's upbringing and education.

GROWING UP Boys generally experience more freedom and less discipline than girls, reflecting the machismo of the larger society. The mother usually

Students of a grammar school in San José.

acts as the chief disciplinarian in the family. Girls are taught to manage the household, while boys are taught to do the outdoor tasks, such as chopping wood and herding cattle. Many lower-class children in urban areas begin work at an early age to help to support the family.

EDUCATION Costa Rica boasts a literacy rate of 96 percent, the highest in Central America. This is the result of the long-standing priority that the Costa Rican government has placed on its education system. In the 1869 constitution Costa Rica became one of the first countries in the world to make education compulsory and free. This progressive program was paid for largely through coffee revenues. Since the 1970s Costa Rica has devoted about a quarter of the national budget to education.

Schooling is compulsory through the ninth grade for children between the ages of 6 and 15. This includes six years of primary education and three years of a basic secondary education. Students who pass their examinations after three years can choose to take two years of specialized course work. They may study academic subjects, agriculture, or various technical subjects. There are six universities in Costa Rica and several regional colleges. Many students from upper-middle- and upper-class families go abroad to study at a university in the United States or Europe.

COURTSHIP AND MARRIAGE   Although girls are still more restricted than boys in their social activities, dating couples are common these days. Couples typically enjoy an engagement of two or three months before getting married. The night before the wedding, the bride's family hosts a party for relatives and friends. Everyone brings a gift for the bridal couple, and they enjoy several hours of drinking and dancing. The wedding usually takes place in a church, with a traditional Roman Catholic ceremony, after which the bride's family hosts another reception for the wedding party.

OLD AGE AND DEATH   Costa Rican culture increasingly emphasizes the advantages of youth, but people still feel an obligation to care for their aging parents, either by sending them money or taking them into their homes. Once a person dies, the legal requirement is that the funeral must be held within 24 hours, as the body of the deceased is not embalmed. Information about the death and details of the funeral are placed in the newspaper or broadcast on television. As many family members as possible gather for the funeral service. It usually takes place in a church, after which the mourners accompany the casket to the cemetery. Many Costa Ricans prefer to be interred in mausoleums rather than buried in the ground.

Funerals in Costa Rica can be very emotional because Costa Ricans have very close family ties and also because mourners are afforded little time to deal with the death due to the quick funeral proceedings.

Young people choose their marriage partners according to age, status, and educational level. They also value their family's approval of their mate.

79

RELIGION

THE 1949 CONSTITUTION states that Roman Catholicism is the official religion of Costa Rica, but it also guarantees freedom of conscience and religious practice to all other denominations and religions. Catholicism is taught in primary and secondary schools, so its residual influence remains strong. Nevertheless, Costa Ricans tend to be casual about religious observances. For many Ticos, Catholicism serves as little more than an observance of ritualistic milestones such as baptism, first communion, weddings, and funerals.

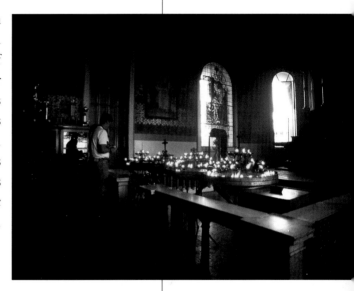

CATHOLICISM

Indications of a religious background pepper the speech of Costa Ricans. Many people say, "Go with God," to someone leaving on a trip or even running a simple errand. In response to any inquiry about their health, many will reply, "Fine, thanks to God." When expressing hopes about future events, they will conclude their comments with "Si Dios quiere," which means, "God willing."

They also often thank someone for a gift or favor by saying, "May God repay you." Despite such common expressions of faith in God, most Costa Ricans are not very fervent believers. Few people, besides elderly people and young girls, go to confession or take communion more often than once a year.

CULT OF THE SAINTS Although the people have a relatively weak religious culture, many believe in the powers of Roman Catholicism's many saints.

Above and opposite:
Worshippers in the Basilica of Our Lady of the Angels offering their prayers and pledges.

Inside a cathedral. Statues of Jesus and the saints are placed on altars, and people stop to pray or light a candle as a form of worship and reverence.

Most pray to one or more saints for intervention or protection in their daily lives. The saint most commonly appealed to is probably the Virgin Mary, the mother of Jesus. Other popular saints include those who are associated with a particular situation, such as traveling or the protection of infants and children. Believers express their devotion to the saints by placing small statues or pictures of the saints in their homes or cars.

SPIRITUAL REVIVAL During the last few decades the Roman Catholic Church in Costa Rica has been undergoing a movement of spiritual revival. Several thousand Ticos have become followers of an evangelical, charismatic movement. The Church terms this movement Spiritual Renovation, although some people refer to it as Catholic Pentecostalism. Believers may speak in tongues, engage in prophesy, and be physically overcome with spiritual utterances and movements.

The move toward spiritual revival within the Catholic Church can be seen in part as a competitive response to the rising influence of evangelical Protestantism in Costa Rica and all of Latin America. Fundamentally, the movement reflects an effort by the Church to engage Ticos more deeply in their faith.

In conjunction with the budding revival of the 1970s, some members of the Church leadership rejected both Communist and liberal economic development philosophies and began to advocate liberation theology, which emphasizes the need for social and political reforms within society.

PLACES OF WORSHIP

Places of worship vary in their degrees of opulence or simplicity, from the beautiful Basilica of Our Lady of the Angels (Basílica de Nuestra Señora de los Angeles) in Cartago to the simple thatch-roofed evangelical church in a small village. Universal features of Roman Catholic churches, regardless of their size or luxury, include statues and pictures of saints.

Protestant churches also vary in style. Many of the evangelical churches are newer and simpler in style, reflecting not only the lower socioeconomic status of some of the congregations but also their belief that the church is "made up of people instead of walls."

The holy image of *La Negrita*, displayed in the Basilica of Our Lady of the Angels. Many Ticos honor the image and believe it has healing powers.

OTHER RELIGIONS

Although Catholicism enjoys its status as Costa Rica's official religion, the constitution grants freedom to other religions as well. Protestants form the second largest religious group, from mainstream Methodists and Baptists to the more charismatic Pentecostal denominations such as the Assemblies of God.

Other religions include Jehovah's Witnesses, a few Chinese folk religions, Judaism, and some indigenous group religions. One-third of the Costa Rican Chinese population is affiliated with the Catholic Church. There are also some remnants of African religious traditions on the Caribbean coast.

FOLK BELIEFS

Today's Ticos are not as superstitious as their parents and grandparents were. Nevertheless, many still believe that certain people have the power to do good or evil. They may attribute the source of such power to magical, psychic, or supernatural forces. Some Ticos even seek the advice of *brujos* (BROO-hos), or sorcerers, and *curanderos* (koo-rahn-DAY-rohs), or healers, whom they ask to predict future events or to cure illnesses.

Some Costa Ricans regularly exercise preventive measures to counteract the possible effects of evil. They may burn incense on Tuesdays and Fridays, when *brujos* are believed to be most active. As water is believed to have supernatural cleansing powers, some people keep a glass of water in the bedroom at night to ward off burglars and illness. While they may not be as superstitious as their forebears, most Ticos still maintain a strong belief in the forces of good or bad luck.

FOLK MEDICINE Costa Ricans tend to mix modern medicine with alternative methods of treatment, such as homeopathic medicine or appeals to saints, spirits, and God. Whatever method of healing they seek, the people believe that faith is the most important ingredient. If their prayers, medicines, or herbs fail to produce hoped-for results, they generally blame themselves for a lack of faith.

An herbal medicine stall in a San José market. Native herbs and flowers are a ready source of folk remedies, used for the treatment of various health ailments.

Folk medicine is more widely practiced in the rural areas, where people have severely limited access to modern health care. Many rural residents attribute serious illnesses and death to the will of God, if not to an evil spell of a *brujo*. If they believe that bad magic has been used against them or their belongings, they may try to purify the affected objects with disinfectants and lemon juice to counteract the spell.

Many Ticos also believe that food and other substances have hot and cold properties. "Hot" foods include coffee, liquor, and pork. It is believed that these can irritate the digestive system. One can "refresh" the liver (believed to be the organ most likely to be affected by "hot" foods) by ingesting "cool" fruits such as pineapple or watermelon. "Cold" foods, on the other hand, include sardines and to some degree all fish or seafood. These foods are likely to cause stomachaches, for which the remedy is a "hot" substance such as chamomile tea.

LANGUAGE

THE OFFICIAL LANGUAGE OF COSTA RICA is Spanish. With the immigrant population, however, English is also fairly common, particularly in certain regions of the country. A few of the indigenous languages remain in active use, although they are spoken only in isolated areas.

SPANISH

There is little regional variation in the spoken Spanish of Costa Rica. Like most Latin Americans, Costa Ricans speak a non-Castilian Spanish—that is, they do not speak the exact Spanish that originated in the Castile region of Spain. The Spanish that Costa Ricans speak has evolved from the language of the first Spanish settlers. Costa Ricans tend to speak Spanish a little more slowly and clearly than many Latin Americans.

Costa Ricans like to embellish their language with elaborate phrases and flowery expressions, especially in writing. They lace their speech with archaic words that make their spoken and written expressions formal and courteous. For example, even in everyday speech, Costa Ricans commonly use the archaic familiar form of you—*vos* (VOHS)—instead of *tú* (TOO), which is more commonly used in the rest of Latin America today.

Such formality is typical of the Costa Rican desire to smooth out the rough edges of social interaction. Flattery and elaborate language are often used, even in a business context. Expressions of courtesy contribute to Costa Rica's image as a warm and friendly society. At the same time, the formality helps to erect certain barriers against unwanted intimacy.

Above: **Tourist signs in Spanish and English at Cahuita National Park.**

Opposite: **Costa Rica boasts of one of the highest literacy rates in the world.**

TICOS Why do Costa Ricans call themselves Ticos? Most people say that the nickname refers to the colonial saying, "We are all *hermaniticos*" (air-mah-nee-TEE-cohs), meaning "little brothers." The substitution of the word *hermanos* (air-MAH-nohs), or "brothers," with the diminutive *hermaniticos* shows the Costa Ricans' historical fondness for diminutizing their words with the suffix *-tico*.

Throughout Latin America people often diminutize their words by adding the suffix *-ito* (EE-to) or *-tito* (TEE-toh). For instance, instead of simply saying *momento* (moh-MAIN-toh), which means "a moment,"

Newspapers are available in Spanish, English, and other languages. Newspapers that publish in Spanish include *La Nacíon*, *La Prensa Libre*, and *La República*.

they will say *momentito* (moh-main-TEE-toh). People use diminutives to soften their speech, making it more affectionate or sympathetic, or to create familiarity.

Costa Ricans especially like to use the diminutive *-ico* or *-tico*, instead of the more common forms *-ito* and *-tito*. For example, where most Latin Americans will say *momentito*, Costa Ricans say *momentico* (moh-main-TEE-coh). The ending also acts as a superdiminutive. While many Latin Americans might diminutize the word *chico* (CHEE-koh), or small, to *chiquito* (chee-KEE-toh) to signify tiny, Costa Ricans often diminutize the word even further by saying *chiquitico* (chee-kee-TEE-koh).

The suffix *-tico* has become an intrinsic part of the way Costa Ricans define themselves. Not only have they adopted it as a nickname, but its very uniqueness is exemplary of the "Costa Rican idiosyncrasy," as they like to say. To describe something that is typical of their culture, they will say that it is *muy tico* (MOOEE TEE-koh), or very Tico. One should note that nationalities are not capitalized in Spanish; hence, Costa Ricans write *ticos* not *Ticos*. Women are *ticas*, the feminine form of the word.

OTHER LANGUAGES

Although Spanish is the official language, English is also widely spoken. A Creole form of English is the most common language on the Caribbean coast of the country. Because of the influx of American immigrants and English-speaking tourists, many Costa Ricans throughout the country speak English as a second language.

Indigenous languages are isolated within the Indian communities. The largest language group is Bribri, spoken by the Indians of the Talamanca region. A few indigenous words have been incorporated into Costa Rican Spanish, mostly in place-names.

In an attempt to preserve their language and cultural roots, the Chinese immigrants to Costa Rica set up a Chinese school in Puerto Limón in the 1950s, where language, writing, calligraphy, and history were taught to their children. The school closed down some years later, however, because of the dwindling number of students.

COMMON EXPRESSIONS

A peculiarity of Costa Rican Spanish is the ubiquitous use of *tiquismos* (tee-KEES-mohs), that is, expressions that are used uniquely by Ticos. Some examples are simply Tico slang words and phrases, such as *buena nota* (BWAY-nah NOH-tah), which literally means "good note" but signifies "cool" or "okay" in Costa Rica. Another expression is *pura vida!* (POO-rah VEE-dah), literally "pure life," but used to say "great!" or "terrific!"

Ticos, like other Latin Americans, also like to use a lot of labels intended as endearments, although they might be considered insults in another country or in less friendly contexts. For example, a Tico might affectionately call someone *flaco* (FLAH-koh) or *gordo* (GOR-doh), meaning "skinny" and "fat," respectively, regardless of the person's appearance. They will openly refer to someone of Chinese descent as *chino* (CHEE-noh), or someone of Afro-Caribbean descent as *negro* (NAY-groh). Young men often call each other *maje* (MAH-hay), which literally means "dummy," though they use it to mean "buddy" or "pal."

Costa Ricans also commonly call each other, even complete strangers, *mi amor* (mee ah-MOR), "my love," as a friendly form of address. They toss around such endearments readily, contributing to their image as a warm and friendly people. The affection is generally well meaning but

SPEECH DIPLOMACY

Costa Ricans always try hard not to embarrass another person or to imply criticism, especially in public. For instance, they are careful not to ask direct questions that may put the other person in a difficult situation. In a work situation, instead of asking, "Have you finished it yet?" a supervisor may say matter-of-factly, "You haven't finished it yet, no?"

superficial. Beneath the ready expression of affection, Costa Ricans are very reserved and cautious about forming close relationships outside their family.

People are expressive in their speech and keep in close contact with friends and family members, aided by the fact that Costa Rica has the best telecommunications system in Latin America.

A POLITE SOCIETY

Expressions of courtesy are important, particularly in the context of greetings and farewells. When greeting an acquaintance, whether in a business or social context, a person always asks about the health of the other person and his or her family before discussing anything else. Social acquaintances will extend an invitation to visit when saying good-bye, even though they do not expect the other party to accept the invitation.

When visiting someone, especially in rural areas, an individual calls out at the door, "*Upe!*" (OO-pay), instead of knocking—there is no real translation of "*upe!*" When entering someone's house, a visitor says, "*Con permiso*" (KOHN pair-MEE-soh), or "With your permission." People also say *con permiso* when passing someone in a crowded room or on a bus.

In Costa Rican households, the first thing that someone says on seeing another family member in the morning is, "How did you awaken?" The standard response is, "Well, fortunately, and you?" Such courtesies exemplify the Costa Rican desire for *quedar bien*, or getting along.

91

Ticos love to gossip, tease each other, and tell jokes, although they are careful to avoid offending someone directly. Costa Rica's criminal code makes it a crime, punishable by a prison sentence, to offend another person's dignity and honor, whether face to face or through a written or spoken message.

THE ALPHABET

Spanish uses a Roman alphabet that has only a few differences from the English alphabet. Traditionally, *ch*, *ll*, and *rr* were considered to be single, separate letters in Spanish. The letter *ñ* is also a separate letter. However all this is now changing and not all Spanish dictionaries treat those letters as separate letters.

NAMES AND TITLES

Costa Ricans follow the Spanish custom of forming a double surname by taking the family surname from both parents. For instance, a young woman by the name of Silvia Calderón Guardia has two surnames: Calderón from her father's family and Guardia from her mother's family. Formally, she is known as Señorita Calderón or as Señorita Calderón Guardia. However, the father's name carries more weight. If she marries a man by the name of Rafael Hurtado Velez, she takes his patrimonial surname and adds it to hers, becoming Silvia Calderón de Hurtado. Formally, she is now known as Señora de Hurtado.

After the first full mention of men's two surnames, they are subsequently usually called by their father's surname, although some may prefer to use

NONVERBAL COMMUNICATION

Costa Ricans do not kiss each other in greeting and good-byes as much as other Latin Americans. Men always shake hands with each other, but women usually greet each other and men with a kiss on the cheek if they are old friends or family or even if they were meeting for the first time. The kiss is executed by touching cheeks and kissing the air. Otherwise, if they were meeting for the first time, they pat each other on the left arm. Costa Ricans do not expect foreigners to be familiar with their custom of greeting one another with a kiss on the cheek.

their double surnames. For example, the current president, Oscar Arias Sánchez, is known as Arias, while Juan Rafael Mora Porras (who served as president in the late 19th century) is referred to as Mora Porras.

In the Caribbean coastal area, English-speaking Ticos use a more casual style of address, calling a person by the first name preceded by Mister or Miss; for example, Silvia Calderón Guardia would be addressed as Miss Silvia.

TITLES Titles are very important in Costa Rica, both socially and professionally. People use titles with their names whenever possible. The most common professional titles are lawyer, architect, engineer, or professor. The most illustrious professional title is that of doctor.

Women do not have to give up their last names when they get married, instead, they add their husband's last name to their own.

Everyone, of course, carries the right to bear the social titles señor (say-NYOR), señora (say-NYO-RAH), or señorita (say-nyoh-REE-tah), which respectively signify Mr., Mrs., and Miss.

A more prestigious social title is still affectionately bestowed on certain people of distinction. Its roots reach back to the minor class divisions of the colonial period. Although everyone was poor during the colonial period, members of the gentry class were called by the honorary title of don (DOHN), or sir. Women of this class were called doña (DOH-nya), or madam. Two examples of men who have been unofficially honored as gentry in the modern democratic republic include the "father of the revolution," Don Pepe Figueres, and another former president, the Nobel laureate Don Oscar Arias.

ARTS

COSTA RICA HAS TRADITIONALLY LOOKED OVERSEAS for artistic inspiration, with Europe as the model. This has restricted the development of an artistic tradition that is uniquely Costa Rican. At one time, many Ticos believed art was something only an educated elite could appreciate. They hesitated to offer real criticism, and, in keeping with the desire for *quedar bien*, mediocre efforts were lavishly praised. During the past few decades, however, the country has enjoyed a flowering of artistic talents. The Meseta towns of Santa Ana and Escazú have become centers of contemporary art. Still, Costa Rica has not produced any artist with the same level of international recognition as the Colombian author Gabriel García Márquez or Mexican muralist Diego Rivera.

Opposite: **A close-up of a colorful native wood carving of a toucan.**

Below: **Children's Last Supper** wood carving by Macedonio Quesada, a contemporary Costa Rican sculptor.

PERFORMING ARTS

As with other forms of artistic expression, the performing arts suffered from a lack of encouragement and active interest until the later half of the 20th century when attitudes began to change, due in part to immigrant playwrights, musicians, and actors from other Latin American countries, and to the participation of young people in arts programs in the schools.

MUSIC The best example of the dramatic change in appreciation for the arts in Costa Rica is the Costa Rican National Symphony. Before 1970 it was a small orchestra that performed a few concerts each year and played primarily European classical music from the 19th century. In the 1970s American Peace Corps worker Gerald Brown was hired to conduct the National Symphony. He revitalized it by recruiting many young foreign musicians to teach their skills to children and adolescents. Costa Ricans are now proud of their National Symphony, which travels around the country to perform concerts, often playing the works of Costa Rican composers. The symphony has also toured internationally and has performed at the White House in Washington, D.C., and at the United Nations in New York City.

Costa Rican composers include Julio Mata Oreamuno, who composed *Suite Abstracta* (soo-EE-tay ahb-STRAK-tah) and the operetta *Toyupán* (toh-yoo-PAHN), and Julio Fonseca Gutiérrez, who composed a symphony, *Fantasía Sinfónica* (fan-tah-SEE-ah seen-FOH-nee-kah), inspired by Costa Rican folk songs. Also noteworthy is César Nieto, who wrote a ballet, *La Piedra del Tóxil* (lah pee-AID-rah del TOH-heel).

DANCE Ticos love to dance. Outside the concert halls, young people enjoy listening to American rock music, but for dancing, they love Latin and Caribbean rhythms. Every town has at least one dance hall or cantina where people dance to *cumbia* (COOM-bya), salsa, merengue, and lambada, and do the Costa Rican swing.

Instrumentation in popular music usually consists of the marimba and guitar. On the Caribbean coast, drums and banjos prevail, beating out the rhythmic *sinkit* (SEEN-keet) and the *cuadrille* (kwah-DREE-yay). The latter is a maypole dance in which the participants each hold the end of a brightly colored ribbon tied to the top of a bare tree trunk or pole. As they dance, they intertwine the ribbons, braiding them down the pole.

Indigenous dances such as the *Danza del Sol* (DAHN-sah del sohl), or Dance of the Sun, and the *Danza de la Luna* (DAHN-sah day lah LOO-nah), or Dance of the Moon, have been preserved by the Chorotega Indians. They have also popularized the musical instruments used in these dances, including the *chirimía* (che-ree-MEE-yah), or oboe, and the

Young girls outside a ballet school.

The National Theater in San José is the grand setting for concerts, dramas, and symphonic performances.

quijongo (kee-HOHN-goh), which is a single-string bow with a gourd resonator.

The Boruca Indians still perform the *Danza de los Diablitos* (DAHN-sah deh los dee-ah-BLEE-tohs), or Dance of the Devils. The music of the Boruca, the *talamanca* (tah-lah-MAHN-kah), has continued to evolve as they have gradually replaced their traditional flutes and drums with guitars and accordions. One such traditional instrument is the *dru mugata* (droo moo-GAH-tah), a small potato-shaped instrument made of beeswax, with a mouthpiece and holes resonating with a soft, deep sound.

THEATER So popular is the theater in Costa Rica today that some say the country has more acting companies per capita than any other nation in the world. The dramatic arts received a boost in the early 20th century when drama was established as part of the school curriculum. The most important source of inspiration, however, was provided by the influence of playwrights and actors from Chile and Argentina who immigrated to Costa Rica around 1900.

San José offers the greatest selection of dramatic arts. From the National Theater to the numerous smaller theaters, Ticos can watch comedy, drama, mime, and puppet-theater productions. In the capital city theatergoers also have opportunities to watch international productions in addition to local and national performances.

LITERARY ARTS

The most significant ingredient in Costa Rican literature has been *costumbrismo* (cohs-toom-BREES-moh), or local color. Novelists and short-story writers have tried to depict the lives and local settings of campesinos and agricultural workers, often writing in a campesino dialect. One such essayist from the first half of the 20th century was Joaquín García Monge, a journalist and teacher who published the journal *Repertorio Americano* (ray-pair-TOHR-yoh ah-may-ree-KAH-noh), or *American Repertory*. The journal was significant because it attempted to form a common Central American identity through the formation of critical and informative dialogue. García also wrote the first important Costa Rican novel, the landmark *El Moto* (el MOH-toh), published in 1900.

Aquileo J. Echeverría is known as Costa Rica's national poet. In the late 1800s he gained recognition throughout Central America for his observations in metrical verse about his fellow Ticos. His best-known collection of poems, *Concherías* (cohn-chay-REE-yahs), describes the Costa Rican landscape and people.

The country's best-known writers today include Alberto Cañas, a journalist, essayist, and novelist; Alfonso Chase, considered to be the country's finest young prose writer; and Carmen Naranjo, whose works are studied in Latin American literature classes in the United States and who is well known throughout Central America. All of them focus on modern themes, although in different styles.

The interior of the National Theater. Costa Rica's various art forms have traditionally been influenced by European writers and artists.

99

Sculptures in front of the Banco Nacional de Costa Rica in San José.

VISUAL ARTS

Costa Ricans looked to European painters and sculptors, largely dismissing the works of local talent, until the late 1920s, when Costa Rican painters began to draw on their own culture and landscape for inspiration. Calling themselves the Group of New Sensibility, these painters became more experimental in their styles, breaking out of the rigidity of conventional artistic expression. They succeeded in developing the first uniquely Costa Rican art style, identified by their depiction of local landscapes, villages, cobblestone streets, and adobe houses.

One of the finest sculptors of the Group of New Sensibility, Francisco Zuñigo, created *Maternidad* (mah-tair-nee-DAD), or Maternity, a stone image of a child being nursed by its mother. The sculpture now stands outside a maternity clinic in San José. Critics were not kind in their comments about the work when the artist unveiled it, however, and Zuñigo was so offended that he moved to Mexico.

Foremost among the painters in the landscape movement was Teodorico Quiros. He painted the impressionistic *El Portón Rojo* (el por-TOHN ROH-ho), or The Red Gate, which hangs today in the Museum of Costa Rican Art. Other members of this group include Manuel de la Cruz, a Picasso-style expressionist; Enrique Echandi, who was influenced by his studies in Germany; and Fausto Pacheco, Margarita Bertheau, and Luisa Gonzáles de Sáenz. In the 1950s painters turned to abstract expressionism and scorned the art of the 1920s as an art of *casitas* (cah-SEE-tahs), or "little houses."

The painters of today are finally achieving recognition beyond the borders of Costa Rica, with their more independent renditions of modernist and contemporary art. Isidro Con Wong, from Puntarenas, is a poor farmer turned painter who has won international acclaim for his style of magic realism. He started painting by using his fingers as a brush and the red paste of the achiote seed as his medium. His paintings now hang in several museums in the United States and France.

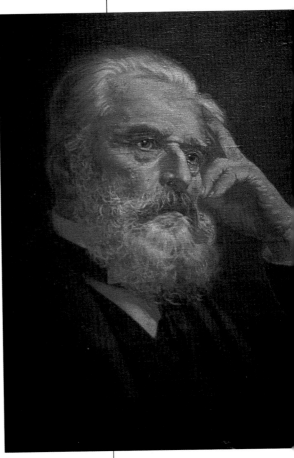

José Joquín Rodriguez, a painting by Emilio Span, displayed at the Museum of Costa Rican Art.

Leonel González, in Puerto Limón, paints images of the black residents of the town silhouetted against colorful and striking backgrounds. Another contemporary painter, Roberto Lizano, is well known for his irreverent abstract portrayals of the Roman Catholic hierarchy.

Folk ceramic art depicting typical countryside life in Costa Rica.

FOLK ARTS

In Costa Rica remnants of pre-Columbian art are relatively scarce in comparison with other areas in Central America where the larger Mayan and Aztec civilizations existed. Costa Ricans value the artifacts that they have found, however, including large statues from the northwestern part of the country and small art works of carved stone and gold. Such rare artifacts are preserved in Costa Rica's National Museum. Indigenous Costa Ricans (most likely the Chorotegas) also produced jade figurines as well as large granite spheres that continue to mystify archaeologists.

The indigenous population has only recently begun to influence the artistic development of Costa Rica, with pre-Columbian art becoming a source of inspiration during the 20th century. Pottery crafted in Nicoya, for instance, follows the traditional craft of the Chorotega Indians. The Boruca Indians create carved balsa-wood masks representing supernatural beings. They also make the decorated gourds that are used in the *quijongo* (kee-HOHN-goh).

The best-known example of Costa Rican folk art is the oxcart, or *carreta* (ka-REH-tah), with its colorful designs and brightly painted wheels. The oxcarts were originally used to transport coffee beans over the mountain roads to the Pacific port of Puntarenas for export. The journey typically took 10 to 15 days. During the rainy season the roads became muddy bogs, so the Costa Ricans devised a solid wheel without spokes that could cut through the mud without becoming stuck. The solid faces of the wheels inspired the wife of a cart maker in San Ramón to design the first decorated *carreta* around the beginning of the 20th century. The idea quickly became a popular custom, and farmers began to take personal pride in their imaginative carts. In the beginning the *carreta* designs consisted primarily of geometric patterns and starbursts, set off by black-and-white accents. Later, artists began to add intricate flowers, leaves, vegetables, faces, and even miniature landscapes.

Farmers added to the overall impact of the *carreta* by creating a unique "song" for each vehicle. A metal ring placed on the wheel would strike the hubcap as the cart bumped along the road, producing a distinctive chime.

The painted oxcart is the most common form of folk art in Costa Rica.

LEISURE

MOST OF COSTA RICAN SOCIETY is guided by an ethos that places the value of leisure higher than that of work. This does not mean that Ticos do not appreciate labor, but rather that a job is generally perceived as a means to attain a certain level of leisure. While work is necessary to earn a living, leisure is the key to enjoying one's life.

SPORTS

Young men participate in sports more actively than the rest of the population, although this is changing. Older men generally feel that it is inappropriate for them to play soccer, for instance, although upper-class men might play tennis or golf in private social and recreational clubs. Middle- and upper-class women with leisure time are more active in today's world, taking up some form of exercise as a means of recreation or of losing weight. They swim or play golf or tennis at private clubs.

SOCCER This is by far the most popular sport in Costa Rica, although it is primarily a spectator sport as it is usually young working-class men who actually participate in the game. Ticos passionately follow the sport, called *fútbol* in Latin America, at the local, national, and international levels. Every town, small or large, has at least one soccer team. Teams in the smallest leagues arrange their matches by broadcasting challenges to other teams over the radio. The major cities and larger towns all have special arenas for soccer games and other sporting events.

OTHER SPORTS Among the working class, bicycle racing inspires enthusiasm among fans and participants. Team sports such as

Above: **Men playing a game of checkers.**

Opposite: **Anglers fishing for sailfish at Drake's Bay at Osa Peninsula. The waters surrounding Costa Rica teem with life and provide the perfect setting for the popular activity of sport fishing.**

basketball and volleyball are more popular among upper- and middle-class boys who play for their school teams. Baseball is especially popular in Puerto Limón, where teams are organized and funded by large private businesses.

Men of all social and economic levels enjoy playing pool, be it at the *pulpería* (general store) or in private clubs. Water sports are also popular, especially with tourists. Europeans and North Americans, in particular, now recognize the spectacular advantages of Costa Rica's natural environment for white water rafting, surfing, windsurfing, and sport fishing. As a result, the Tico interest in such aquatic pursuits is growing too.

The national passion for soccer is such that any open field or vacant lot can be converted instantly into a soccer pitch.

Hundreds of miles of coastline provide numerous beaches for surfing. Surfers are challenged by the ever-changing formation of sandbars that reshape the coastline every year. Game fishermen angle for large fish such as tarpon, mahimahi, and snook that swim upstream from the ocean into the rivers and freshwater lakes.

OTHER SPECTATOR SPORTS Boxing and wrestling rank as favorite spectator sports among working-class Tico men. Even though Ticos are generally peace loving, they love to watch professionals fight each other in a controlled setting.

Although cockfights are now illegal, the authorities sometimes allow a cockfight to take place, levying a special tax that goes to charity. People of all social classes enjoy watching horse races, bicycle races, and automobile or motorcycle racing.

THE PURSUIT OF LEISURE

In addition to sporting activities, Ticos enjoy spending their leisure hours socializing, listening to the radio, or watching television. Most of their time is spent with members of their immediate or extended families, although increasing numbers of Costa Ricans are joining professional or social clubs and organizations. Leisure time does not necessarily have to be constructive. Many delightful hours are spent simply whiling the time away. Ticos laughingly refer to such idle time as "killing the snake." The expression is derived from a standard excuse given by plantation workers who disappear into the jungle when they are supposed to be working. Whenever the foreman demands to know where they have been, their tongue-in-cheek answer would be that they were out "killing the snake."

SUNDAY ACTIVITIES In small towns Sunday is the liveliest day of the week. People dress in their best clothes, and some attend Mass, after which they stroll around town, window-shop, eat ice cream, visit family members, or watch a soccer match. They may travel to a nearby community to visit family members or take a day trip to the beach or mountains. Adolescents socialize with their friends, going dancing or to the movies or just hanging out.

Surfing by Witch's Rock at Playa Naranjo in Santa Rosa National Park.

In larger towns the streets are usually quietest on Sundays, although the soccer stadium is sure to be packed with zealous fans. Urban residents often leave town on Sundays to visit family members or spend a day relaxing at the beach or at a resort.

MEN'S DIVERSIONS Working-class men spend most of their leisure time away from home. After work and on their days off, they may spend hours chatting with friends on street corners or in *pulperías* and cantinas. They also go to the movies, play pool, and attend sporting events. Gossip, alcohol, and pool take up much of a Tico's leisure time.

RADIO The radio remains a popular source of entertainment. It is the most widespread form of media communication, with one radio for every 1.2 persons in 1999. Agricultural workers take a transistor radio with them while they work, women working at home listen to the radio while they do their chores, and office workers leave the radio on at their desks. For many rural residents the radio is their primary connection to the outside world. Costa Rica has over 100 radio stations. Most play popular music interspersed with news, advertisements, and soap operas. Others offer classical music or religious, cultural, or educational programs.

TELEVISION This powerful medium has become increasingly widespread. In 2006 there were 139 television sets for every 1,000 people. Some Ticos blame television for the loss of traditional values and family interaction. Instead of talking together on the front porch or in the kitchen as in previous decades, families often spend their evenings watching television.

Costa Rican TV programs include soccer games, news broadcasts, music videos, game shows, and handicraft and hobby shows such as gardening or sewing. Most television programming, however, consists of old cartoons, situation comedies, movies imported from the United States, or soap operas from Mexico. In recent years, though, there has been an increased access to cable television, especially in the Meseta Central. Channels such as Music Television and HBO are now producing shows specifically for the Latin American market.

The pulpería, *or general store, also serves as a major social center for a village or neighborhood. Costa Ricans, especially men, gather at the* pulpería *to watch television, play pool, listen to the jukebox, drink alcohol, and gossip.*

STORYTELLING

The telling of stories within a group setting is a more traditional leisure-time activity. Television has largely replaced this classic form of social interaction, however, and few young people are familiar with the traditional stories. Some older residents of the Caribbean coastal areas like to gather and exchange stories. Many of the tales originated in West Africa but have been molded by the experiences of blacks in the Caribbean and the Americas. A favorite character, for example, is Anansi the Spider, a trickster who uses his wits to outsmart larger and stronger animals. While Anansi is usually represented as a spider, he can also be portrayed as a little bald man who plays a fiddle and performs magic.

FESTIVALS

THE COSTA RICAN CALENDAR is chock-full of holidays and festivals; only a few are mentioned here. On most holidays the majority of Costa Ricans enjoy a day off from work or school. Although there may be public festivities such as parades or special ceremonies, many Ticos head for the beaches or the mountains to spend a day of leisure with their family or friends. Some Costa Ricans complain that their country cannot afford the profusion of public holidays that some countries enjoy. Many business people argue that productivity suffers enough from the holidays they have. Even in the 1970s it was calculated that each weekday holiday costs the country nearly $2 million in lost productivity. Legislators have responded to the concern by moving some holiday observances to the following Sunday or by cutting out others altogether.

Left: **Holidays are for relaxation and time spent with the family.**

Opposite: **Girls taking part in the festivities of the Carnival parade in Puerto Limón.**

MAJOR HOLIDAYS AND FESTIVALS

January 1	New Year's Day
March 19	Saint Joseph's Day (patron saint of San José)
March or April	Holy Week (Thursday and Friday before Easter itself)
April 11	Juan Santamaría's Day (commemorating the national hero who fell fighting William Walker in 1865)
May 1	Labor Day
June 15	Corpus Cristi (religious event)
June 29	Saints Peter and Paul's Day
July 25	Guanacaste Day (annexation of Guanacaste province)
August 2	Our Lady of the Angels Day (patron saint of Costa Rica)
August 15	Mother's Day/Catholic Feast of the Assumption
September 15	Independence Day
October 12	Columbus Day
November 2	Day of the Dead
December 1	Abolition of the Armed Forces
December 8	Immaculate Conception/Holy Communion Day
December 25	Christmas Day
December 28–31	San José celebrations

RELIGIOUS HOLIDAYS

Costa Rica's lack of fervent religious devotion is reflected in the people's increasing secularization of religious holidays. Although processions and Masses still take place, most Costa Ricans use religious holidays as an excuse to take a day off from work or school, or simply to have a party with family and friends.

HOLY WEEK The week preceding Easter has long been one of the most important religious commemorations in Costa Rica. The Roman Catholic Church celebrates the Christian holiday with great ceremony. The observance of Holy Week, however, has become increasingly secularized in the past few decades. More than fifty years ago businesses closed for the latter half of the week, and a large ceremonial procession would take place in the streets. From Wednesday through Saturday morning people did not drive their cars and buses did not operate. Today some businesses close, but more as a vacation than as a religious observance. Fewer people

San Antonio de Escazú festival featuring cowboys and oxcarts.

participate in religious processions, and many urban residents leave town for a holiday. In many small towns and villages Holy Week continues to be observed with elaborate processions, rites, and feasts. Some Ticos like to travel to such places to experience the more traditional ceremonies.

CHRISTMAS   Ticos celebrate Christmas with much more glitz and enthusiasm than most Latin Americans. Indeed, Christmas in Costa Rica has all the commercial glitter of the North American holiday season. By early December, Ticos crowd the stores and send greeting cards to family,

GOOD FRIDAY IN THE CARIBBEAN

Caribbean Ticos relieve the solemnity associated with Good Friday by playing practical jokes. Calling it Judas Day, they adopted the tradition from the Miskitu Indians of Nicaragua.

On Judas Day, a favorite trick is stealing an item such as a chair, washtub, or chamber pot off someone's porch, taking it to the center of town and leaving it under an effigy of Judas. Victims of jokes must retrieve their property themselves, while the townspeople jeer and laugh at them. Victims who are too embarrassed to go themselves might pay children to retrieve the items for them.

friends, and business associates. Children send their Christmas wish lists to Niño Jesus, the Christ Child, who will send their presents through his messenger, Santa Claus. The *gordo* (GOR-doh), or fat Christmas lottery, promises wealth to hopeful ticket buyers. A few days before Christmas many Ticos decorate a cypress tree or a dried coffee branch with bright strips of paper, colored balls, small figurines, and lace.

The only truly authentic Costa Rican tradition is the nativity scene. Families construct elaborate miniature villages around the traditional manger, which remains empty until Christmas Eve. These displays, which may take up a corner of the living room, mix colorful elements of religious and secular symbolism, both past and present.

On Christmas Eve, Ticos exchange visits in a whirl of eating, drinking, dancing, and gift giving. At midnight they place the Christ Child in the manger. The family might attend Midnight Mass, after which adults celebrate until dawn. Children may go to bed a bit late on Christmas Eve but rise eagerly in the morning to open their gifts. Tamales, rectangular pieces of cornmeal dough filled with seasoned meat or beans, are traditionally eaten during the Christmas

Children regard Santa Claus as a gift-bearer for the Christ Child.

holidays. Stuffed turkey is also served, and it is believed that the Spanish introduced this dish and other exotic foods such as corn, sweet potatoes, and chili peppers to Europe around or soon after the time of Columbus's discovery of the New World.

SECULAR HOLIDAYS

Ticos enjoy any excuse to gather together and indulge in music, food, and alcohol. Most of Costa Rica's public holidays offer an excellent opportunity to indulge the social spirits of its people. In addition to national holidays, many towns celebrate local holidays. For instance, Puerto Limón celebrates a nationally recognized Columbus Day, in a spirit akin to a carnival, as *El Día de la Raza* (el dee-a day la RAH-sah), the Day of the Race, celebrating not only the human race but also the heritage of Spanish America.

NEW YEAR'S DAY The most festive part of the New Year's holiday is, of course, New Year's Eve, when Ticos gather to drink and dance the night away. It is one of the most boisterously celebrated holidays of the year, serving as the climax of the weeklong festivities from Christmas to the New Year. On New Year's Day, Catholics attend Mass, after which a costume parade takes place and people break open Santa Claus piñatas, which are colorful, hollow papier-mâché containers filled with candy and small gifts. Horse shows and nonviolent bullfights are held as well.

MAYPOLE On the Caribbean coast, English-speaking Costa Ricans celebrate the spring festival known as the maypole. The Miskitu Indians

CELEBRATION OF THE DEVILS

The Boruca Indians celebrate the *Fiesta de los Diablitos* (fee-AIS-tah day los dee-ah-BLEE-tohs), or Celebration of the Devils, on December 30 each year. The festival has less to do with devils and more to do with the Spanish—the Indians reenact the war between the Spanish invaders and the indigenous people during the 16th-century Spanish conquest of the region. In the festival celebration, though, the Indians win.

of Nicaragua brought the maypole, or *palo de mayo* (PAH-loh day MAH-yoh) with them when they migrated to the Caribbean coast of Costa Rica in the 1940s and 1950s. The festival has roots in old Celtic celebrations in Europe. Now the tradition has spread throughout several African-American populations along the Caribbean coast of Central America, from Belize to Panama. The maypole is celebrated not only in May, but also often in June, just for the sheer enjoyment of it.

A tree is decorated with lots of gifts, candies, sweets, and a bottle of liquor. Everyone dances around the tree, after which boys start climbing the tree and taking down the presents and sweets. The revelers eat and drink, with the adults imbibing lots of *chicha* (CHEE-cha), or sugarcane liquor.

Sometimes people follow tradition and decorate a tall, slender post instead. They attach a number of colorful ribbons to the top, and celebrants each take the end of a ribbon. Then they dance around the pole in a special way, braiding the ribbons as they go.

Another feature of the festival is the climbing of a tall pole covered in a greasy substance to obtain prize money at the top. Observers laugh and cheer while the contestants struggle to climb the pole. After someone finally collects the prize, the singing and dancing continue.

DAY OF THE DEAD

Celebrated on November 2, the Day of the Dead is the traditional Latin American festival for the dead—although Halloween, on October 31, has become increasingly popular in recent years due to commercial and popular influences from the United States. Every year on the Day of the Dead Costa Ricans celebrate with candy skulls and bone-shaped breads. They carry flowers to cemeteries and mausoleums and decorate the graves of their departed family members. The deceased are so faithfully remembered that they retain an almost palpable presence in Costa Rican society.

COMMUNITY CELEBRATIONS AND STREET FAIRS

Individual communities celebrate *fiestas cívicas* (fee-AIS-tahs SEE-vee-kahs) and *fiestas patronales* (fee-AIS-tahs pah-troh-NAHL-ays), civic festivals and patron saints' festivals. The secular civic festival inspires a great community spirit every year in the smaller towns and villages. The patron saints' festivals are religious in nature, but feature many of the same activities as the secular celebrations.

In addition to the annual civic festival, towns and villages also hold *turnos* (TOOR-nohs), or street fairs, to raise money for churches, schools, or other causes. The *turno* is an elaborate, noisy affair attended by fun seekers of all ages. The fair fires off at dawn with explosions of rockets and usually continues all weekend. Attractions and events generally include mechanical rides, fireworks, and fund-raising bingo games, lotteries, or raffles. The air pulses with marimba music or perhaps with the spirited notes of a band with a guitar, accordion, and maracas. A neighboring town usually attends with its soccer team to play a fiesta game. The inevitable beauty contest takes place, and a queen is chosen from among the young women whose pictures have been published in the newspapers in the days leading up to the fair.

The colorful and lively Spanish dances that are performed by Costa Rican dancers lend an air of gaiety to any festival or celebration.

117

FIESTAS CÍVICAS The annual civic festival fosters a tremendous amount of community spirit, especially in the smaller towns and villages. In the weeks prior to the fiesta, organizers visit each household with a truck, collecting contributions of livestock, grain, food, or cash. The town council may donate electric power for the event, and local businesses often donate money, labor, and materials. The *fiesta cívica* is a grander version of the *turno*. Food vendors offer tripe soup, rice cakes, beef stew, and other special dishes. Music fills the air, and people dance, play bingo, or go on carnival rides. Bullfighting is a popular event, especially in the weeklong *fiestas cívicas* in San José.

FIESTAS PATRONALES The date and style of the patron saints' festivals vary according to the saint and the town. The fiesta usually includes a procession in which participants carry an image of the saint through the streets. Other activities may involve rodeos, dancing, feasting, fireworks, and bullfights (although these days the bull is not harmed or killed).

The most important saint's day for the country as a whole is that of *Nuestra Señora de los Angeles* (noo-AYS-trah-seh-NYOR-rah day los

BULLBAITING

Costa Rican bullfights, or *corridas* (koh-REE-dahs), are nonviolent in the sense that the bulls are not killed. Young men enter a ring with a small bull. They tease the bull by chasing it and trying to avoid getting hurt themselves. They engage in this "bullbaiting" without the protection of swords or spears, in an attempt to prove their skill and show off their machismo. The events provide as much comic relief as admiration for the daring of the young men. Someone occasionally gets hurt, either from drinking too much alcohol beforehand or from taking too many risks with the bull.

AHN-hay-lays), or Our Lady of the Angels, the patron saint of Costa Rica. The history behind her patronage dates back to August 2, 1635, when a tiny black stone image of the Virgin Mary was discovered in Cartago and was removed from the site, only to reappear miraculously. This happened several times. The statuette became known as *La Negrita* (la nay-GREE-tah) and is believed to bestow miraculous healings.

The Basilica of Our Lady of the Angels in Cartago was built as a shrine in her honor on the site where the statue was discovered. The basilica was destroyed in the 1926 earthquake but was rebuilt in a Byzantine style. Its grandeur and its position as the residence of *La Negrita* make it the most famous church in Costa Rica. Inside the church is a special chapel dedicated to *La Negrita*, where pilgrims who have been cured of illnesses leave gifts in her honor. People walk from all parts of Costa Rica to visit the cathedral.

FOOD

EATING AND DRINKING MAKE UP an important part of life in Costa Rica. Almost every social gathering includes alcohol, which is usually served with *bocas* (BOH-kahs), or appetizers. Bocas, also called *boquitas* (boh-KEE-tahs), consists of foods such as black beans, chicken stew, or potato chips. Costa Rican food is not particularly spicy, but is well seasoned. In addition to the local cuisine, Ticos in the larger towns and cities can eat out at a variety of international restaurants, including Italian, French, Middle Eastern, Spanish, Peruvian, North American, German, Mexican, Korean, Chinese, and Japanese.

Above: **Workers preparing pastries at a bakery.**

Opposite: **Food vendors in Costa Rica.**

TICO-STYLE COOKING

A middle- or upper-class kitchen in the Meseta Central is relatively modern, equipped with an electric stove and refrigerator. Urban kitchens generally have a few cupboards, shelves along the wall, and a small wooden table used for food preparation. A cement or stone sink with a cold-water tap often serves as the washbasin for both laundry and dishes.

Many rural residents still cook with firewood on a cast-iron stove that sits on a wooden or cement platform, with a narrow chimney poking through the roof. These people continue to use woodstoves even when electricity is available, simply because they prefer the taste of food cooked over a wood fire. As recently as 1980, two-thirds of all Costa Rican households cooked with wood fuel instead of electricity.

In the small towns and villages of the Caribbean region, most residents also cook over wood fires. Modern ovens are relatively scarce, except in restaurants. In many households the kitchen is separated from the main house so that the inhabitants can avoid the smoke and heat of the fires.

The women often build the fire in the open air. When it gets hot enough, they place a heavy cooking pot over the fire and put the food inside, such as bread or pudding dough. Then they heap wood coals or hot coconut husks on top of the lid to provide heat for the top of the food. The cook must have much experience and skill to maintain a constant heat so that the food emerges neither burned nor soggy. If the fire is too hot or if too many burning husks are placed on the lid, the bread will be burned on the outside and uncooked in the middle.

COMMON INGREDIENTS

These jalapeño chili peppers, harvested in the mountainous areas of Cervantes and Zarcero in Costa Rica, are not as hot as the Mexican varieties.

Costa Rican cuisine, especially in the Meseta Central, relies heavily on starches and red meat, although the ingredients vary according to social class and urban or rural residence. Rice, beans, plantains, and potatoes are the staples. Except for those who live on the Caribbean coast, Ticos prefer beef and pork to fish, even though they have plenty of access to fresh seafood.

Costa Rican food is very tasty and judiciously flavored without being spicy hot. Ticos season their food with a mixture of dry spices and sauces that give the food a typical Costa Rican flavor. Some of the most commonly used spices include fresh coriander and mild jalapeño chili peppers.

Costa Rican food combines the indigenous ingredients of the Americas with ingredients and flavorings introduced by the Spanish. A popular dish of Spanish origin is *olla de carne* (OH-yah-day KAR-nay), a classic beef and vegetable stew made with beef, yucca (a tuberous vegetable), potatoes, corn, plantains, squash, and other vegetables.

A tidy, well-stocked fruit stand along the road.

Gallo pinto (GAH-yoh PEEN-toh), or spotted rooster, is one of the most common Costa Rican dishes and is eaten primarily for breakfast, along with eggs. It consists basically of black beans and white rice, seasoned with onions, sweet peppers, and fresh coriander.

Throughout the country, Ceviche, or Seviche, is a popular way of eating seafood as an appetizer. Shrimp, or shellfish, or perhaps sea bass is marinated in lemon juice, onion, garlic, and coriander, which "cooks" it.

A multitude of fruits are produced in Costa Rica. Fruits grow plentifully in the diverse tropical climates and are widely used in juices, desserts, and side dishes. In addition to melons, pineapples, mangoes, passion fruit, guava, apples, and papaya, Ticos also enjoy a host of even more exotic fruits. The fragrant rose apple, for instance, smells like a rose and is best used as a preserve, though it can be eaten fresh in small quantities. The sweet Costa Rican star apple looks like the Malaysian starfruit; when cut in cross-section, it resembles a star. One of the most popular fruits is the *pejibaye* (pay-hee-BAI-yay), a shiny orange fruit with black stripes and yellow flesh. The *pejibaye* cannot be eaten raw, but is a common ingredient in Costa Rican cooking.

Like many Latin Americans, Ticos love sweet pastries, breads, and cakes. Typical deserts are pastel de tres leches (pah-STEL day trays LAY-chays), the three-milk cake, and arroz con leche (ah-ROHS cohn LAY-chay), which is a rice pudding.

123

A family making tamales. After its introduction to the region, each Central American country has adapted the tamale to suit its own taste.

INDIGENOUS INFLUENCE The Costa Rican diet is primarily based on Spanish cuisine but also displays the strong influence of indigenous ingredients, especially corn. The pre-Columbian Indians of Central America centered their lives and cultures around corn, which served as a flour (cornmeal) as well as a vegetable. For instance, they ground dried corn into a fine meal to make tortillas, a very thin pancake, usually topped with meat or cheese.

The Chorotega Indians of Costa Rica also cook tamales, which is one of the most important festival foods for Costa Ricans. They are rectangular pieces of dough made from beaten corn, lard, and spices, filled with a variety of ingredients and wrapped in a corn husk or banana leaf and steamed. The Aztecs introduced tamales throughout Central America, and each country prepares them in its own special way. In Costa Rica the Chorotega Indians stuff their tamales with tomatoes, pumpkin seeds, sweet peppers, and deer or turkey meat.

124

CUISINE OF THE MESETA CENTRAL
People in the highlands subsist largely on the traditional staples of rice, beans, plantains, and corn. Beef is the preferred meat, but chicken and pork are also eaten.

CARIBBEAN DIET Ticos living along the Caribbean coast eat a lot of rice, potatoes, beans, cabbage, and corn, as well as cucumbers, carrots, tomatoes, beets, and peanuts. These ingredients are mostly imported from the inland regions of Costa Rica. Breadfruit and coconut are locally available. Coconut milk is a popular ingredient for many dishes and beverages. Many agricultural workers gather much of their own food through a combination of hunting, fishing, and farming. Coastal residents enjoy fish much more than the rest of the Costa Rican population, although they eat beef, chicken, and pork as well. Turtle meat and turtle eggs are considered delicacies, although it is illegal to collect turtles or their eggs from the beaches. A typical dish of the Caribbean coastal region is "rundown," a runny, stewlike dish put together with whatever ingredients are available. It always includes coconut milk, some kind of meat or fish, and vegetables. The vegetables are generally the most variable part of the dish, but may consist of potatoes, cassava, plantains, or bananas.

BEVERAGES Costa Ricans drink excellent coffee, since it is one of their main agricultural products. They like to drink it strong, very sweet, and served with hot milk. Campesinos even give coffee to children and babies because they consider it nourishing.

A dish of black beans.

With the profusion of fresh fruits available throughout the year, Ticos also drink a variety of juices at any time of the day. The most common fruit juices are made from mango, papaya, pineapple, watermelon, cantaloupe, passion fruit, and blackberry. Especially in the coastal areas, people like to punch a hole in the top of a coconut and drink the refreshing coconut water. (This is not coconut milk, which is prepared from grated coconut meat.)

Sodas and *batido* (bah-TEE-doh) abound. A *batido* is fruit juice mixed with milk or water. *Horchata* (or-CHA-tah) is a rather milky beverage made from cornmeal and cinnamon. The preference for such beverages clearly demonstrates Costa Ricans' love of sweets. *Agua dulce* (AHG-uah DOOL-say), or sweet water, is another such drink, containing nothing more than boiled water and brown sugar. The term *refresco* (ray-FRAIS-koh), "refreshment," is a more general term for a beverage.

ALCOHOL This is essential at most Costa Rican social gatherings and festivities. Although Ticos like to drink, they do not approve of drunkenness. Two of the cheapest and most widely available liquors are *chicha* (CHEE-cha) and *guaro* (GUA-roh), which are made from sugarcane alcohol, although *chicha* is sometimes made from fermented corn. Beer and wine are also popular, as are hard liquors such as rum, vodka, and gin. Tico beer is usually light-colored and Ticos like to add salt and lime to it.

Coconuts are popular for their natural water and the milk derived from grating and squeezing the white flesh of the fruit.

HOLIDAY FOOD AND DRINK

Perhaps the most popular holiday or festival food are tamales, the flavorful indigenous food described above. These are a traditional part of the Costa Rican Christmas feast and are also served at weddings, fiestas, and other special occasions.

In Puerto Limón holiday diners also eat pork cracklings and *mondongo* (mohn-DOHN-goh), a soup made with the tripe (stomach) of a cow. People drink wine, punch, and liquor. They also make their own ginger beer, a favorite nonalcoholic beverage for women, though they can add wine to it if they want.

The *refresco* stand is a welcome sight on a hot day.

MEALTIMES

For campesinos and many lower-class Costa Ricans, ordinary meals are repetitive and unvarying in their composition. Rice and beans are the primary components of nearly every meal, and *gallo pinto* practically

---

A TASTE OF TRADITION

One of the most famous specialty foods in Costa Rica is *el casado* (el cah-SAH-doh), which means "married man." It got its name in the early days when wives would pack lunch for their husbands, who were generally the only ones in the family who went out to work. Served in many restaurants, this dish consists of a platter of rice and beans accompanied by a variety of side dishes such as cabbage and tomato salad; fried plantains; chicken, fish, or beef; and maybe even a fried egg or fried yucca.

constitutes the national dish. *Café* (cah-FAY), or coffee, as the morning meal is called, tends to be relatively simple. The midday meal is the heaviest, followed by a light supper in the evening. Ticos snack frequently and drink lots of sweet soda and coffee throughout the day.

In the rural areas campesinos rise before dawn and eat a simple breakfast of coffee and *gallo pinto* with a fried egg, or they may have tortillas and sour cream. The women wait on the men during the meal, while nibbling at their own breakfast on the side. The midday meal usually consists of tortillas or white bread, black beans and rice, plantains, and possibly a bit of meat or sausage, with *agua dulce* to drink. The evening meal is the same.

The urban middle class eats a more varied diet, relying more on processed and convenience foods. They might begin the day with a bowl of packaged cereal or an egg, and freshly made fruit juice, along with white bread and coffee with hot milk. The midday meal usually includes a soup, beefsteak or chicken, plantains, bread or tortillas, a green salad, cooked vegetables, eggs, milk, a fruit dessert, and coffee. The evening meal is very light, consisting of sandwiches or leftovers from lunch. *Batidos*, fruit juice mixed with milk or water, usually accompany most meals.

MARKETPLACES

Costa Ricans purchase their food from three basic types of markets. The traditional marketplace is the open-air market with its many rows of individual stalls. Most towns and villages also have a *pulpería*, or general store, which sells basic goods and supplies. Larger towns and cities in Costa Rica have modern supermarkets with well-stocked shelves.

The traditional marketplace is crowded with close-set stalls offering, for example, hot tortillas and tamales, live chickens or pigs, and colorful cut flowers. Shoppers thread their way through row upon row of fresh

fruits and vegetables. Vendors also sell finished products such as leather goods, clothing, handmade baskets, toys, hammocks, and dishes. These markets are found either outdoors or in large enclosed buildings.

The *pulpería* serves as the corner grocery in city neighborhoods or as the general store in smaller towns and villages. The walls behind the counter are lined with shelves displaying a wide variety of dry goods, processed and canned foods, and staples, including rice, oil, sugar, salt, rum, cleaning supplies, and hardware. Brooms, coils of rope, and woven bags hang from the ceiling. A single shopkeeper usually manages the store, and the goods are generally fixed at a certain price.

Other options for food in urban areas are offered by individual specialty stores and produce stands, common in towns and large cities. People often go to the neighborhood bakery or dairy store, or stop by a corner produce stand on their way home from work.

Saturday mornings are the busiest time for the marketplaces, where vendors peddle their wares in the open.

ARROZ GUACHO (STICKY RICE)

3 teaspoons vegetable oil
1 pound (0.5 kg) lean short pork ribs, cut into 1-inch cubes
1 bunch fresh cilantro, chopped
1 clove garlic, crushed
½ cup red bell pepper, chopped
½ cup onion, chopped
Salt and pepper to taste
1 pound (0.5 kg) uncooked long grain rice, rinsed and drained

Heat vegetable oil in a saucepan over medium high heat. Add the pork and stir for about three minutes to brown, then add water to cover two inches above the meat. Bring to a boil, before lowering the heat. Simmer for 20–30 minutes until pork is tender. Stir in cilantro, garlic, red bell pepper, onions, salt, and pepper. Add uncooked rice and more water to one inch above the pork ribs, stirring occasionally until rice is cooked. This recipe makes eight servings.

ARROZ CON LECHE (RICE PUDDING)

1 cup uncooked long grain rice
½ cup water
6 cups milk, divided
1 cup canned evaporated milk
½ teaspoon vanilla extract
2 sticks cinnamon, cracked
1 teaspoon fresh nutmeg
1 cup canned sweetened condensed milk
½ cup raisins

Add the uncooked rice, water, four cups of milk, evaporated milk, vanilla extract, cinnamon, and nutmeg to a medium saucepan and bring to a boil over high heat, stirring occasionally. Simmer over low heat for five minutes; then add sweetened condensed milk and simmer for about 15–20 minutes. Stir in the remaining two cups of milk gradually. Stir until mixture thickens. Add raisins and cook for 10 more minutes. Serve chilled or at room temperature. This makes eight servings.

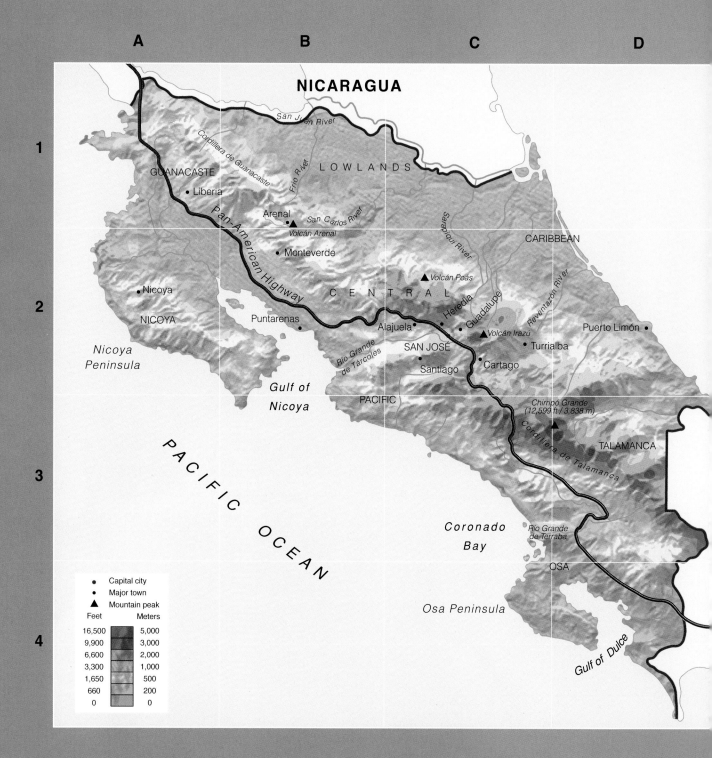

NICARAGUA

San Juan River

Frío River

San Carlos River

Sarapiquí River

Reventazón River

GUANACASTE

Cordillera de Guanacaste

L O W L A N D S

CARIBBEAN

• Liberia

Arenal

▲ Volcán Arenal

▲ Volcán Poás

Pan-American Highway

• Monteverde

C E N T R A L

Heredia

Guadalupe

• Nicoya

Puntarenas

Alajuela

▲ Volcán Irazú

Puerto Limón •

NICOYA

SAN JOSÉ

Turrialba

Nicoya
Peninsula

Rio Grande
de Tárcoles

Santiago

Cartago

Gulf of
Nicoya

PACIFIC

Chirripó Grande
(12,599 ft / 3,838 m)

Cordillera de Talamanca

TALAMANCA

P A C I F I C   O C E A N

Coronado
Bay

Rio Grande
de Terraba

OSA

Osa Peninsula

Gulf of Dulce

Legend

● Capital city
• Major town
▲ Mountain peak

Feet		Meters
16,500		5,000
9,900		3,000
6,600		2,000
3,300		1,000
1,650		500
660		200
0		0

E

N

MAP OF COSTA RICA

CARIBBEAN
SEA

PANAMA

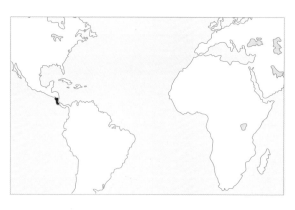

ECONOMIC COSTA RICA

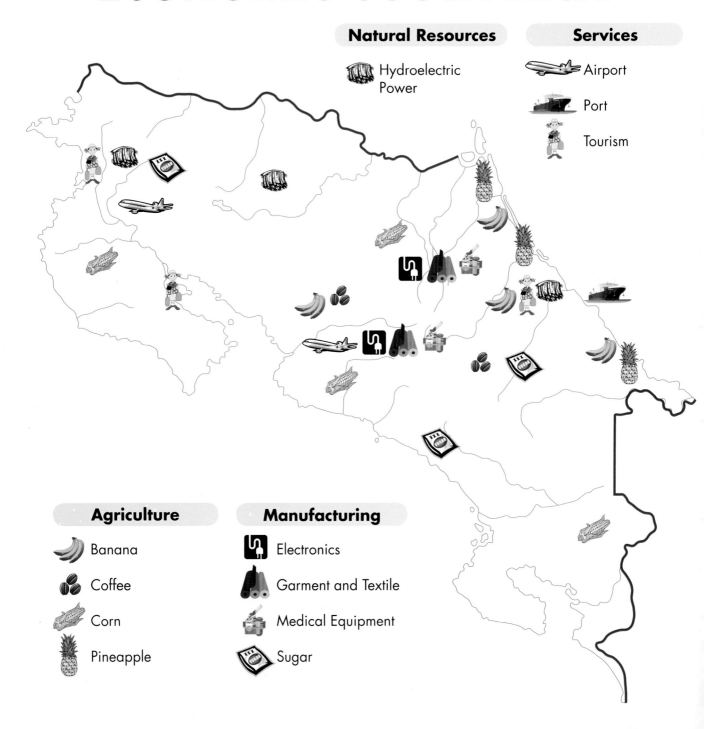

Natural Resources

Hydroelectric Power

Services

Airport

Port

Tourism

Agriculture

Banana

Coffee

Corn

Pineapple

Manufacturing

Electronics

Garment and Textile

Medical Equipment

Sugar

ABOUT THE ECONOMY

OVERVIEW

Costa Rica's stable economy depends on tourism, agriculture, and electronics exports. Its major economic resources include fertile land and well-educated people as well as its strategic location that allows easy access to North and South American, European, and Asian markets. Standard of living is relatively high compared with its Central American neighbors, and the country's political stability continues to attract foreign investment.

GROSS DOMESTIC PRODUCT (GDP)

$19.38 billion (2005 estimate)

GDP GROWTH

4 percent (2005 estimate)

LAND USE

Arable land 4.4 percent; permanent crops 5.87 percent; others 89.73 percent (2005 estimates)

CURRENCY

Costa Rican colón (CRC)
Notes: 500, 1,000, 2,000, 5,000, 10,000 colón
Coins: 5, 10, 20, 25, 50, 100 céntimos
1 USD = 517 CRC (2007)

NATURAL RESOURCES

Hydropower

AGRICULTURAL PRODUCTS

Coffee, pineapples, bananas, sugar, corn, rice, beans, potatoes, beef, timber

MAJOR EXPORTS

Coffee, bananas, sugar, pineapples, textiles, electronic components, medical equipment

MAJOR IMPORTS

Raw materials, consumer goods, capital equipment, petroleum

MAIN TRADE PARTNERS

United States, Netherlands, China (including the special region of Hong Kong), Japan, Venezuela, Mexico, Brazil (2005)

WORKFORCE

1.82 million (2005 estimate)

UNEMPLOYMENT RATE

6.6 percent (2005 estimate)

INFLATION RATE

13.8 percent (2005 estimate)

EXTERNAL DEBT

$5.049 billion (2005 estimate)

CULTURAL COSTA RICA

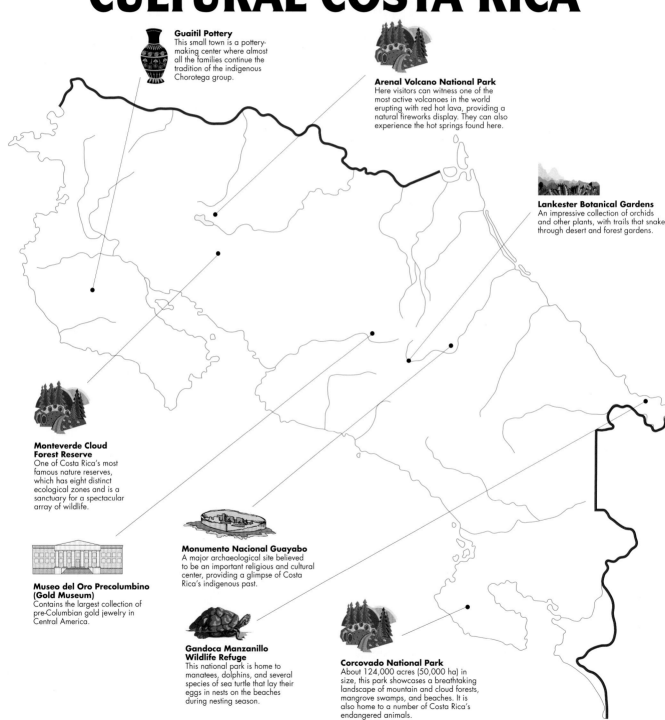

Guaitil Pottery
This small town is a pottery-making center where almost all the families continue the tradition of the indigenous Chorotega group.

Arenal Volcano National Park
Here visitors can witness one of the most active volcanoes in the world erupting with red hot lava, providing a natural fireworks display. They can also experience the hot springs found here.

Lankester Botanical Gardens
An impressive collection of orchids and other plants, with trails that snake through desert and forest gardens.

Monteverde Cloud Forest Reserve
One of Costa Rica's most famous nature reserves, which has eight distinct ecological zones and is a sanctuary for a spectacular array of wildlife.

Museo del Oro Precolumbino (Gold Museum)
Contains the largest collection of pre-Columbian gold jewelry in Central America.

Monumento Nacional Guayabo
A major archaeological site believed to be an important religious and cultural center, providing a glimpse of Costa Rica's indigenous past.

Gandoca Manzanillo Wildlife Refuge
This national park is home to manatees, dolphins, and several species of sea turtle that lay their eggs in nests on the beaches during nesting season.

Corcovado National Park
About 124,000 acres (50,000 ha) in size, this park showcases a breathtaking landscape of mountain and cloud forests, mangrove swamps, and beaches. It is also home to a number of Costa Rica's endangered animals.

ABOUT THE CULTURE

OFFICIAL NAME
Republic of Costa Rica

FLAG DESCRIPTION
Five horizontal bands of blue (top), white, red (double width), white, and blue, with the coat of arms in a white elliptical disk on the hoist side of the red band; above the coat of arms a light blue ribbon contains the words AMERICA CENTRAL, and just below it near the top of the coat of arms is a white ribbon with the words REPUBLICA COSTA RICA.

TOTAL AREA
19,730 square miles (51,100 square km)

CAPITAL
San José

ETHNIC GROUPS
White (including mestizo) 94 percent, black 3 percent, indigenous Amerindian 1 percent, Chinese 1 percent, other 1 percent (2005 estimates)

RELIGIOUS GROUPS
Roman Catholic 76.3 percent; evangelical 13.7 percent; Jehovah's Witness 1.3 percent; other Protestant 0.7 percent; other 4.8 percent; none 3.2 percent (2005 estimates)

BIRTH RATE
18.32 births per 1,000 Costa Ricans (2006 estimate)

DEATH RATE
4.36 deaths per 1,000 Costa Ricans (2006 estimate)

AGE STRUCTURE
0 to 14 years: 28.3 percent; 15 to 64 years: 66 percent; 65 years and over: 5.7 percent (2006 estimates)

MAIN LANGUAGES
Spanish (official), English

LITERACY
People aged 15 and above who can both read and write: 96 percent (2005 estimate)

LEADERS IN POLITICS
José María Figueres Ferrer—president (1953–58, 1970–74)
Oscar Rafael Arias Sánchez—president (1986–90, 2006–)
Rafael Angel Calderón Fournier—president (1990–94)
José María Figueres Olsen—president (1994–98)
Miguel Angel Rodríguez Echeverría—president (1998–2002)
Abel Pacheco de la Espriella—president (2002–06)

TIME LINE

IN COSTA RICA	IN THE WORLD
13,000 B.C.	
Earliest archaeological record of settlers in Costa Rica.	
1,000 B.C.	
Olmec migrants arrive from Mexico.	**753 B.C.**
	Rome is founded.
	116–17 B.C.
	The Roman Empire reaches its greatest extent, under Emperor Trajan (98–17).
	A.D. 600
	Height of the Mayan civilization
	1000
1502	The Chinese perfect gun powder and begin to
Christopher Columbus lands in Costa Rica.	use it in warfare.
	1530
	Beginning of transatlantic slave trade organized by the Portuguese in Africa.
	1558–1603
1561	Reign of Elizabeth I of England
The Spanish successfully colonize Costa Rica.	
1563	
The city of Cartago is founded.	
	1620
1737	Pilgrims sail the *Mayflower* to America.
San José is founded.	**1776**
	U.S. Declaration of Independence
	1789–99
	The French Revolution
1808	
Coffee is introduced as a cash crop.	
1821	
Central America gains independence from Spain.	
1823	
Costa Rica joins the United Provinces of Central America.	
1835	
San José is agreed upon as the capital.	

IN COSTA RICA	IN THE WORLD
1838 Costa Rica becomes fully independent.	
1856 Battle of Santa Rosa against William Walker.	
1859 President Juan Mora Porras ousted from power.	**1861** The U.S. Civil War begins.
1870s First banana plantations established.	**1869** The Suez Canal is opened.
1889 First election to be won by an opposition party.	**1914** World War I begins.
1941 Social security and health system is established.	**1939** World War II begins. **1945** The United States drops atomic bombs on Hiroshima and Nagasaki.
1949 Women and people of African descent are given the right to vote.	**1949** The North Atlantic Treaty Organization (NATO) is formed.
1987 President Oscar Arias Sánchez is awarded Nobel Peace Prize for regional peace plan.	**1991** Breakup of the Soviet Union **1997** Hong Kong is returned to China. **2001** Terrorists crash planes in New York, Washington, D.C., and Pennsylvania.
2002 For the first time in Costa Rican history, presidential elections are forced into a second round.	**2003** War in Iraq begins.
2004 Corruption by three former presidents is exposed.	
2006 Oscar Arias Sánchez wins a neck-and-neck presidential election race.	

GLOSSARY

Adiós
Hello or good-bye.

batido (bah-TEE-doh)
A drink made of fruit blended with water or milk.

bocas (BOH-kahs)
Appetizers.

brujos, brujas (BROO-hos, BROO-has)
Sorcerers; witches.

campesinos
Peasants, small farmers.

choteo (cho-TAY-oh)
Mockery, especially of pretensions or boastfulness.

con permiso (KOHN pair-ME-soh)
A polite phrase meaning "with your permission."

curanderos (koo-rahn-DAY-rohs)
Herb doctors or faith healers.

gringo
A nonpejorative term to describe a person from the United States.

hidalgo
Member of the gentry class in colonial times.

indígenas (een-DEE-hay-nahs)
Indigenous population of Indian origin.

josefinos (ho-say-FEE-nohs)
Residents of San José.

machismo
Exaggerated masculine attitude and daring behavior, mostly exhibited by young men.

maje (MAH-hay)
This literally means "dummy" but is often used to mean "buddy" or "pal."

marianismo (mah-ree-ahn-EES-moh)
Concept of feminine ideal emphasizing self-sacrifice and submission to husband and family.

mestizo
Person of mixed white and indigenous ancestry.

plebeyos (play-BAY-yohs)
"Commoners," or people from the lower class, during colonial times.

pulpería (pool-pay-REE-ah)
General store that serves as a social gathering place.

quedar bien (kay-DAR bee-EN)
Social art of getting along with others and leaving a good impression.

refresco (ray-FRAIS-koh)
Fruit juice mixed with milk or water.

FURTHER INFORMATION

BOOKS

Biesanz, Mavis H., Richard Biesanz, Karen Z. Biesanz. *The Ticos: Culture and Social Change in Costa Rica*. Boulder, CO: Lynne Rienner Publishers, 1998.

Booth, John A. *Costa Rica: Quest for Democracy (Nations of the Modern World: Latin America)*. Boulder, CO: Westview Press, 1998.

Collard, Sneed B. *Monteverde: Science and Scientists in a Costa Rican Cloud Forest*. London: Franklin Watts, 1997.

Evans, Sterling. *The Green Republic: A Conservation History of Costa Rica*. Austin, TX: University of Texas Press, 1999.

Fisher, Frederick. *Costa Rica (Festivals of the World)*. Milwaukee, WI: Gareth Stevens Publishing, 1999.

Haynes, Tricia. *Costa Rica (Major World Nations)*. Langhorne, PA: Chelsea House Publications, 1998.

Helmuth, Chalene. *Culture and Customs of Costa Rica (Culture and Customs of Latin America and the Caribbean)*. Westport, CT: Greenwood Press, 2000.

Morrison, Marion. *Costa Rica (Enchantment of the World. Second Series)*. Danbury, CT: Children's Press, 1998.

Schafer, Kevin. *Costa Rica: The Forests of Eden*. New York: Rizzoli, 1996.

WEB SITES

Best Places: Costa Rica—general information. www.bestplacescostarica.com
Costa Rica Conservation Trust: Socially Responsible Conservation. www.conservecostarica.org
Rainforest Alliance: Innovative Solutions for Global Conservation. www.rainforest-alliance.org
Viva Costa Rica! Online guide to Costa Rica travel and living. www.vivacostarica.com

FILMS

The Living Eden's: Costa Rica—Land of Pure Life. Abc/Kane Productions, 2000.
Exploring Costa Rica—Colors, Creatures and Curiosities. Trailwood Films, 2001.

MUSIC

Afro Limonese: Music from Costa Rica. Lyrichord, 1991.
Costa Rica: Calypso. Buda Records, 1999.
Music of Costa Rica. Arc Music, 2005.

BIBLIOGRAPHY

Barry, Tom. *Costa Rica: A Country Guide*. Albuquerque, NM: Interhemispheric Resource Center, 1991.

Biesanz, Richard, Karen Zubris Biesanz, and Mavis Hiltunen Biesanz. *The Costa Ricans*. Prospect Heights, IL: Waveland Press 1982 (updated 1988).

Costa Rica in Pictures. Minneapolis, MN: Lerner Publications, 1988.

Insight Guides, *Costa Rica*. Singapore: Apa Publications, 1994.

Lara, Sylvia, Tom Barry, and Peter Simonson. *Inside Costa Rica: The Essential Guide to Its Politics, Economy, Society and Environment*. Albuquerque, NM: Interhemispheric Resource Center, 1995.

Lefever, Harry G., *Turtle Bogue: Afro-Caribbean Life and Culture in a Costa Rican Village*. London and Toronto: Associated University Presses, 1992.

Lonely Planet. *Costa Rica*. London: Lonely Planet Publications Pty Ltd, 2004.

Nelson, Harold D. *Costa Rica: A Country Study*. Washington D.C.: U.S. Government Printing Office, 1983.

Caribbean Environment Programme: Promoting regional cooperation for the protection and development of the marine environment of the Wider Caribbean Region. www.cep.unep.org

Central Intelligence Agency World Factbook (select Costa Rica from country list). www.cia.gov/cia publications/factbook

Costa Rica—Food. www.costarica.com/Home/Culture/Food

Costa Rica National Parks National System of Conservation Areas. www.costarica-nationalparks.com

Costa Rica Tourism and Travel Bureau. http://www.costaricabureau.com

Costa Rica Travel Information and Tips. www.infocostarica.com

Countries and Their Cultures: Listing of Costa Rican Web sites. www.everyculture.com

Mongabay—Tropical Rainforest Conservation. www.mongabay.com

The Nature Conservancy. www.nature.org

The Tico Times Online Edition: www.ticotimes.net

Water for Life. http://outreach.ecology.uga.edu/wfl/home.htm

INDEX

143